God's Image

The circle shape, representing God, is reflected like a mirror. It is God's image reflected in man.

Sin

This diamond represents sin and its absolute corruption. The sharp edges and corners contrast the perfect wholeness of the circle.

Justification

These triangles are perfectly matched, which speaks to the idea of being made complete only by God's righteousness in us.

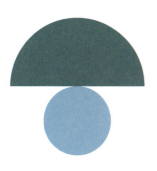

Sanctification

The circle here represents the Spirit of God, which supports the half circle that symbolizes mankind becoming more and more like God.

Perseverance and Glorification

The quarter circles represent the saints glorifying God. They are united, mirroring the circle that represents God.

Eternity

This ring shape represents eternity because it has no beginning and no end. It is infinite.

"Paul Tripp is a trusted, fatherly guide to shepherd us through the core doctrines of Christianity. This readable, Scripture-soaked resource is simply fantastic. I can think of no finer tool for helping instruct our teenagers in the basic truths of the gospel. I hope churches, parents, and teachers everywhere will immediately put it into use!"

Gavin Ortlund, President, Truth Unites; Theologian in Residence, Immanuel Nashville, Tennessee

"As a parent, I deeply value any resource that helps guide those who are growing to know and love God through his word amid the complexities of faith and life. *12 Truths Every Teen Can Trust* does just that—offering an important, accessible, and thoughtful presentation of core Christian beliefs. This book breaks down timeless truths into clear, manageable ideas that resonate with the challenges many teenagers face today. It not only builds a strong spiritual foundation for young minds but also provides parents with a trusted tool to support meaningful conversations about faith."

Amy Gannett, Writer and Bible teacher, The Bible Study Schoolhouse; Founder and Creator, Tiny Theologians; author, *Fix Your Eyes*

"Being a part of a church plant has reminded me that new disciples need careful consideration and instruction. This book is a great resource to help guide young believers in their journey with Christ. Build your life on these truths!"

Quina Aragon, author, *Love Has a Story*

"Paul Tripp is a gift from God to the church, and this book will bring clarity and grace to those looking for solid ground to stand on. Highly recommended!"

Sam Allberry, Associate Pastor, Immanuel Nashville, Tennessee; author, *One with My Lord*

12 Truths Every Teen Can Trust

Books by Paul David Tripp

40 Days of Faith
40 Days of Grace
40 Days of Hope
40 Days of Love
A Quest for More: Living for Something Bigger Than You
A Shelter in the Time of Storm: Meditations on God and Trouble
Age of Opportunity: A Biblical Guide to Parenting Teens
Awe: Why It Matters for Everything We Think, Say, and Do
Broken-Down House: Living Productively in a World Gone Bad
Come, Let Us Adore Him: A Daily Advent Devotional
Dangerous Calling: Confronting the Unique Challenges of Pastoral Ministry
Do You Believe: 12 Historic Doctrines to Change Your Everyday Life
Everyday Gospel: A Daily Devotional Connecting Scripture to All of Life
Forever: Why You Can't Live Without It
How People Change (with Timothy S. Lane)
Instruments in the Redeemer's Hands: People in Need of Change Helping People in Need of Change
Journey to the Cross: A 40-Day Lenten Devotional
Lead: 12 Gospel Principles for Leadership in the Church
Lost in the Middle: Midlife and the Grace of God
Marriage: 6 Gospel Commitments Every Couple Needs to Make
My Heart Cries Out: Gospel Meditations for Everyday Life
New Morning Mercies: A Daily Gospel Devotional
New Morning Mercies for Teens: A Daily Gospel Devotional
Parenting: 14 Gospel Principles That Can Radically Change Your Family
Reactivity: How the Gospel Transforms Our Actions and Reactions
Redeeming Money: How God Reveals and Reorients Our Hearts
Relationships: A Mess Worth Making (with Timothy S. Lane)
Sex in a Broken World: How Christ Redeems What Sin Distorts
Suffering: Gospel Hope When Life Doesn't Make Sense
Sunday Matters: 52 Devotionals to Prepare Your Heart for Church
War of Words: Getting to the Heart of Your Communication Struggles
Whiter Than Snow: Meditations on Sin and Mercy

12 Truths Every Teen Can Trust

Core Beliefs of the Christian Faith That Will Change Your Life

Paul David Tripp

WHEATON, ILLINOIS

12 Truths Every Teen Can Trust: Core Beliefs of the Christian Faith That Will Change Your Life
© 2025 by Paul David Tripp
Published by Crossway
    1300 Crescent Street
    Wheaton, Illinois 60187
All rights reserved. No part of this publication may be reproduced, stored in a retrieval system, or transmitted in any form by any means, electronic, mechanical, photocopy, recording, or otherwise, without the prior permission of the publisher, except as provided for by USA copyright law. Crossway® is a registered trademark in the United States of America.
Cover design: David Fassett
Cover images: Cover and interior geometric shapes originally designed by Ordinary Folk
First printing 2025
Printed in China
The text of *12 Truths Every Teen Can Trust* has been adapted from Paul David Tripp, *Do You Believe? 12 Historic Doctrines to Change Your Everyday Life* (Crossway, 2021).
Scripture quotations are from the ESV® Bible (The Holy Bible, English Standard Version®), © 2001 by Crossway, a publishing ministry of Good News Publishers. Used by permission. All rights reserved. The ESV text may not be quoted in any publication made available to the public by a Creative Commons license. The ESV may not be translated in whole or in part into any other language.
All emphases in Scripture quotations have been added by the author.
Hardcover ISBN: 979-8-8749-0538-5
Epub ISBN: 979-8-8749-0540-8
PDF ISBN: 979-8-8749-0539-2

Library of Congress Cataloging-in-Publication Data
Names: Tripp, Paul David, 1950- author. | Tripp, Paul David, 1950- Do You Believe?
Title: 12 truths every teen can trust: core beliefs of the Christian faith that will change your life / Paul David Tripp.
Other titles: Twelve truths every teen can trust
Description: Wheaton, Illinois: Crossway, [2025] | Includes index. |
Audience: Ages 13–18
Identifiers: LCCN 2024059834 (print) | LCCN 2024059835 (ebook) | ISBN 9798874905385 (hardcover) | ISBN 9798874905392 (pdf) | ISBN 9798874905408 (epub)
Subjects: LCSH: Theology, Doctrinal—Juvenile literature. | Christian Life—Biblical teaching—Juvenile literature.
Classification: LCC BT77 .T7649 2025 (print) | LCC BT77 (ebook) | DDC 230—dc23/eng/20250409
LC record available at https://lccn.loc.gov/2024059834
LC ebook record available at https://lccn.loc.gov/2024059835

Crossway is a publishing ministry of Good News Publishers.

RRD			34	33	32	31	30	29	28	27	26	25
15	14	13	12	11	10	9	8	7	6	5	4	3	2	1

Contents

Introduction   *vii*

1   Scripture   *1*

2   God   *13*

3   God's Holiness   *27*

4   God's Sovereignty   *41*

5   God's Power   *55*

6   God's Creation   *67*

7   God's Image   *79*

8   Sin   *91*

9   Justification   *103*

10   Sanctification   *117*

11   Perseverance and Glorification   *131*

12   Eternity   *145*

Scripture Index   *157*

Introduction

Everyone loves a great story. Maybe it's *Star Wars, The Lord of the Rings*, or something from the Marvel Cinematic Universe. Stories capture us, entertain us, teach us, warn us, and even change us. Stories can give us courage or make us afraid. Stories can supply us with hope or leave us hopeless. Stories can teach us what is right or tempt us to love what is wrong. Stories can transport us to other worlds or help us understand our own. Stories can lead us toward the light of truth or take us to dark places. Every generation, every culture, every location, and every human is shaped by stories.

You may not know it, but you tell yourself stories. More significantly, in your everyday life, the stories you are telling yourself are the ones you live out. Maybe you're telling yourself the story of your family. Perhaps your story is one of athleticism or physical beauty. Maybe you're telling yourself a story of being misunderstood and rejected. Perhaps it's a story of academic ability and future promise. Maybe in your story, you end up with lots of success and money.

In all this, here's what's so important to recognize: The way you think, what you desire, the things you say, the decisions you make, and the actions you take are all shaped by the story you tell yourself.

There is one story that is better than any story you and I could ever tell ourselves. It is the story that God tells us in his word. When you hold a Bible in your hands, you are holding the greatest story that has ever been or ever will be told. This story has been recorded and preserved for you because God loves you and wants you to know him, and in knowing him, to thrive. In this grand redemptive narrative, you will learn who God is, what life is about, who you are, what went wrong in our world, and how it will get fixed. God's great story has only one hero: Jesus. He is the hope of God's story because he came to fix everything sin left broken. He came as our substitute; he came to do for us and in us what we could never do. Why? So that in him we might find forgiveness, acceptance with God, and the grace of personal transformation.

This book you are about to read is a storybook too. That may confuse you at first because it doesn't read like a story. It doesn't have characters, villains, creatures, and mythical lands. But *12 Truths Every Teen Can Trust* really is a story. This book walks you through twelve core beliefs that God preserved for us in his word. Each of these twelve truths—also known as doctrines—tells you something important about God's great story.

Doctrines are quick summaries of essential things in the biblical story. When you understand these twelve truths, you will know who God is, what life is about, how sin damaged us and this world, and how Jesus entered this world to rescue us and make everything new again. These twelve truths are meant to give you personal identity, meaning and purpose, an inner sense of well-being, courage for today, and hope for the future. They are intended to free you from living for yourself and introduce you to the freedom and joy of living for something and someone much bigger than yourself—God. They are meant to help you recognize right from wrong and worship from idolatry. God recorded and preserved these twelve truths to change you and how you think about everything in your life.

You are reading this book because, by grace, your story has already been embedded in the Bible's incredible story of redemption. This means the biblical story is your story. The Bible's plot—creation, fall, and redemption—is the plot of your personal story. So dig in and discover the core beliefs of the best story ever told.

Here's what you'll find in each of the following twelve chapters:

First, I'll briefly lay out the doctrine we'll be considering in a section titled "What We Believe." These summaries are simplified paraphrases from parts of the Westminster Confession of Faith, a beautiful statement of the truths of the Christian faith from the seventeenth century.

Second, in a section titled "Why We Believe It," you'll see a selection of Bible passages that form a solid foundation for the doctrine we're considering.

Finally, in the "How It Matters" section, I'll give you seven readings that will help you better understand and love the doctrine that is our focus.

May this book help you to understand how to live out your story wherever you are, whomever you're with, and whatever you're facing. And may it cause you to love Jesus and his word more than you ever have before.

1

Scripture

What We Believe

God has revealed himself and perfectly declared his will by committing his truth to writing. This makes Scripture (the Old and New Testaments of the Bible) essential and authoritative. Because it is God's word, it is to be believed, obeyed, and joyfully received. In Scripture, we have all things necessary for God's own glory and for our salvation, faith, and life.

Why We Believe It

The passages below inform the Christian doctrine of Scripture. God has spoken in the Bible, so we believe what he has said there. In the following pages, we'll explore this key doctrine and what it means for us as we follow Christ.

The heavens declare the glory of God,
　　and the sky above proclaims his handiwork.
Day to day pours out speech,
　　and night to night reveals knowledge.
There is no speech, nor are there words,
　　whose voice is not heard.
Their voice goes out through all the earth,
　　and their words to the end of the world.
In them he has set a tent for the sun,
　　which comes out like a bridegroom leaving his chamber,
　　and, like a strong man, runs its course with joy.
Its rising is from the end of the heavens,
　　and its circuit to the end of them,
　　and there is nothing hidden from its heat.
The law of the LORD is perfect,
　　reviving the soul;
the testimony of the LORD is sure,
　　making wise the simple;
the precepts of the LORD are right,
　　rejoicing the heart;
the commandment of the LORD is pure,
　　enlightening the eyes;
the fear of the LORD is clean,
　　enduring forever;

the rules of the LORD are true,
and righteous altogether.
More to be desired are they than gold,
even much fine gold;
sweeter also than honey
and drippings of the honeycomb.
Moreover, by them is your servant warned;
in keeping them there is great reward.

Psalm 19:1–11

I still have many things to say to you, but you cannot bear them now. When the Spirit of truth comes, he will guide you into all the truth, for he will not speak on his own authority, but whatever he hears he will speak, and he will declare to you the things that are to come. He will glorify me, for he will take what is mine and declare it to you.

John 16:12–14

But as for you, continue in what you have learned and have firmly believed, knowing from whom you learned it and how from childhood you have been acquainted with the sacred writings, which are able to make you wise for salvation through faith in Christ Jesus. All Scripture is breathed out by God and profitable for teaching, for reproof, for correction, and for training in righteousness, that the man of God may be complete, equipped for every good work.

2 Timothy 3:14–17

And we have the prophetic word more fully confirmed, to which you will do well to pay attention as to a lamp shining in a dark place, until the day dawns and the morning star rises in your hearts, knowing this first of all, that no prophecy of Scripture comes from someone's own interpretation. For no prophecy was ever produced by the will of man, but men spoke from God as they were carried along by the Holy Spirit.

2 Peter 1:19–21

How It Matters

Throughout this chapter, we'll focus on God's word. The same God who made the world tells us how to live in it. His word is the only place to find true wisdom, which we need every day. Thankfully, God doesn't leave us on our own to figure out the meaning of the Bible. He graciously teaches us what he has written and how it relates to all of life. In love, he warns us about dangers and shines his light into our darkness. For the Christian, God's word is daily food, healthy and sweet as honey.

1. World and Word

Every morning when we get up, we bump into God and come face-to-face with his existence.

He is revealed in the wind and the rain, in the bird and the flower, in the rock and the tree, in the sun and the moon, in the grass and the clouds, in sights, smells, touches, and tastes. Everything that exists is a finger that points to God's existence and glory.

The cycle of the seasons points to his wisdom and faithfulness. The fact that we all see creation's beauty, are warmed by its sun, and are drenched by its rain points us to his love and mercy. The thunderous storms, with crashes of lightning and violent winds, point to the immensity of his power. The created world is a stunning display of the existence and attributes of the one who created it all.

God is so good to build into creation reminders of himself everywhere. He wants us to constantly think of him when we look at the world he created.

But in his infinite wisdom, God knew that creation was not enough. Creation could never teach us to truly know him or ourselves. If we just look at creation, we can't understand the meaning and purpose of life. We can't know the disaster of our sin or the glory of his saving grace. So God gave us the wonderful and amazing gift of his word.

Here's why this is so important: If there were no word of God, then we would be left to ourselves to decide what is true. This would mean that there would be no way of being sure that what we think and believe is right. We wouldn't have any basis to guide our thinking, desires, decisions, words, and actions. But in his grace, God has given us his word so we would know how to live as children of that same grace.

Read: "The unfolding of your words gives light; it imparts understanding to the simple." PSALM 119:130

Reflect: What's your favorite part of God's world (nature) and his word (Scripture)? How do they help you know God more closely?

---

2. Wisdom for Fools

One of the devastating results of sin is that it reduces all of us to fools.

A fool looks at truth and sees falsehood. A fool looks at bad and sees good. A fool ignores God and inserts himself into God's position. A fool rebels against God's wise and loving law, and writes his own rules. A fool thinks he can live on his own, not needing anyone's help.

But here is what is deadly about all of this: A fool doesn't know he is a fool. If a fool isn't given eyes to see his foolishness, then he will continue to think he is wise.

So God, in his grace, did not turn his back on our foolishness and walk away. God looked on foolish humanity with a heart of compassion. He not only sent his Son to rescue fools from themselves but also gave us the wonderful gift of his word. In this way, fools could recognize their foolishness and have a tool by which they could grow in wisdom.

How do you start the search for wisdom? The first steps are not in university classrooms, on the pages of research papers, on popular podcasts, or in the books on the *New York Times* bestseller list. Wisdom begins in the pages of God's word.

You can be highly trained and still be a fool. You can be a well-educated and gifted communicator and still be a fool. You can be successful and famous and still be a fool. You can have social media dominance and still be a fool. You can be a person whom people look to for guidance and still be a fool. But no one is hopelessly trapped in foolishness. Why? Because God, who is the source of all true wisdom, is a God of tender, forgiving, and rescuing grace (1 Cor. 1:18–31).

To all who confess their foolishness and run to him for wisdom, he offers mercy and grace in their time of need.

Read: "The law of the LORD is perfect, reviving the soul; the testimony of the LORD is sure, making wise the simple." PSALM 19:7

Reflect: When you need advice, where do you turn first for ideas, help, or guidance?

---

3. True Confession

I would not know how to live without the wisdom of God's word.

I would not know how to be a responsible man without the wisdom of God's word. I would not know how to be a husband, a father, a neighbor, a friend, a member of the body of Christ, a citizen, or a worker without the Bible.

Without Scripture, I would not know right from wrong. Without the truths of the word, I would not know how to understand and respond to suffering. Without Scripture, I would be confused about who I am and my purpose in life. Without my Bible, I would not know about sin or understand true righteousness. Without God's word, I would not know how to handle money, success, power, or fame.

Without Scripture, I would have no understanding of origins and no concept of eternity. Without God's word, I would have no idea of my need for rescue, reconciliation, and restoration. Without my Bible, I would have no understanding of what it means to love or what I should hate.

Apart from God's word, I would have no wise and holy law to follow. I'd have no amazing grace to give me hope. If it were not for Scripture, I would have no wisdom of any worth to share.

But here's what I have experienced: My Bible is my lifelong friend and companion. My Bible is my wisest and most faithful teacher. My Bible is my mentor and my guide. My Bible confronts me when I am wrong and comforts me when I am struggling.

My Bible is my most treasured physical possession. I know that as long as sin still lives in me, I need divine wisdom. So I approach my Bible every day as a needy and thankful man.

Read: "For with you is the fountain of life; in your light do we see light." PSALM 36:9

Reflect: What is your daily plan for spending time with God in his word and prayer?

---

4. Not Just the Word

Not only do we have the gift of God's word, but we also have the gift of the Holy Spirit. He's the one who guides us, teaching us through his word. As a result, we can know, understand, confess, and repent.

I not only need the content of God's word, but I also need the help of the Holy Spirit. He enables me to understand it. He assists me to apply it, empowers me to live it, and equips me to take its message to others. God rescues me from my foolishness not just by handing me a book but also by giving me himself—and he opens the wisdom of that book to me.

As an author of books, I don't do this. I write a book and move on. Then it's up to the reader to make sense of what I have written. I don't travel to reader after reader, sitting with them as long as it takes, shining light on the things I have written, making sure they understand, and helping them to apply the content of the book to their everyday lives.

But that is exactly what God does. He goes everywhere his word goes. He patiently sits with readers every time they open his book. He teaches them out of his word. God is not only the author of his word, he's also its primary teacher.

When you get the word of God, you also get the God of the word, and that is a beautiful thing.

Read: "Teach me your way, O LORD, that I may walk in your truth; unite my heart to fear your name." PSALM 86:11

Reflect: When reading God's word, in what ways are you inviting the Lord to speak to you? How are you tempted to depend on your own ability to understand the Bible?

5. God's Word Teaches

I remember my days as a seminary student with fondness and thankfulness. By God's grace, I was able to focus three years of my life on one solitary thing: studying God's word. This was a once-in-a-lifetime blessing. I don't know when I have been more thankful and motivated by anything in all of my life.

I soaked it all in. And at the end of each day (and to the suffering of my wife), I repeated to her—in great detail and length—each lecture I had heard. I read long portions to her from dense biblical theology books. I was obsessed with and thrilled by what I was learning. It got me up early in the morning and kept me up late at night. It was just about all I thought and talked about. My mind was blown away by the word of God in a way that it had never been before.

One day after classes, I ran up the steps to our third-floor apartment and said to Luella, "It's not just that I'm learning the content of the Bible and learning theology. But for the first time, I'm learning to think—really, truly think!"

Not only was the Bible opening up to me, the whole world was opening up to me with levels of meaning I had never known before. As I sat day after day studying the word, I was, in fact, sitting at the feet of the Creator of the world. Yes, the word was the tool, but it was held in the hands of the ultimate teacher, my Lord. I was being taught as I had never been taught before, but not just by wise and seasoned professors. I was also being instructed by my Master through the majestic wisdom of his word.

God's word teaches in ways unlike anything else. It teaches you things that you will learn nowhere else. It doesn't just impart knowledge to you—it also forms wisdom in you. It reveals to you the deepest, most profound spiritual mysteries that could ever be considered.

Read: "Oh how I love your law! It is my meditation all the day. Your commandment makes me wiser than my enemies, for it is ever with me. I have more understanding than all my teachers, for your testimonies are my meditation." PSALM 119:97–99

Reflect: What is the difference between mastering God's word and *being mastered* by God's word? Why is that difference so important?

6. Words of Warning

Why are there so many warnings in Scripture? They are there because God loves us.

You see, a warning isn't judgment. If all God intended to do was to judge you, he wouldn't first warn you. Think about how parents constantly warn their children. They first warn them not to touch the hot stove, the lit candle, or the electrical outlet. Later they warn them what is safe to eat and what is dangerous, and down the road they warn them about the dangers of the internet and social media. Every one of these warnings is motivated by tenderhearted parental love.

God is our heavenly Father. And like our parents, he's committed to warning us about the dangers of life in this fallen world. In each warning, he is loving us. Each warning exhibits his patience, faithfulness, wisdom, and grace. Each warning reminds us of his care. Each warning teaches us again that he is ready and willing to forgive and restore. Each warning is a call to trust him and to follow him by faith. Each warning reminds us that our Father is infinitely smarter than us. He really does know better. So we should listen and obey.

You don't want to be like the toddler who refuses to listen to Mommy's warnings and burns his finger on the oven door. You don't want to be like the teenager who blows off her dad's warnings and makes decisions that mess up the rest of her life. God loves us, so he has dotted his word with warnings. With fatherly care he says, "Don't look there, don't say that, don't desire this, don't do that, don't choose that, don't love that, watch out for this."

Don't think you are smarter than God. Don't believe the lie that there will be no cost for ignoring his wise and loving warnings. Every sin, and every mess that follows, is a result of a failure to humbly heed God's warnings. And remember, he not only warns you but also gives you the grace you need to live inside of his warnings.

Read: "Therefore we must pay much closer attention to what we have heard, lest we drift away from it." HEBREWS 2:1

Reflect: Where have you neglected to submit your heart and life to God's loving warnings?

7. Words That Guide

When was the last time you needed to use your cell phone as a flashlight? Maybe you were looking for something in the garage, trying to read a menu at a dimly lit restaurant, or finding something in the backyard at night.

Why did you need the light? Your answer probably includes something about the dark or darkness. As a sinner living with other sinners in a fallen world, you encounter darkness every day. While you may experience Instagram-worthy sunny-day picnic lunches, real life is more like a midnight walk through the woods.

On any given day, you probably encounter more darkness than truth—both in you and around you. So to move forward without danger and get to where you are meant to go, you need something to light your way. No passage gets at this need and God's provision better than Psalm 119:105 (see below).

You need light for your school and your friendships. You need light for your struggles and temptations. You need light to handle difficulties. You need light for when you have been sinned against. You need light for when you feel alone and overwhelmed.

You need light for all the unknowns that will show up on your doorstep tomorrow, the day after tomorrow, and for the rest of your life.

You don't have to grope around fearfully in the darkness. You don't need to bloody your nose and bruise your toes by bumping into trees and tripping over roots. The light of the world has graced you with the light of his word! It will shine around your feet in the midst of the darkness so that you won't stumble and fall.

Read: "Through your precepts I get understanding; therefore I hate every false way. Your word is a lamp to my feet and a light to my path."
PSALM 119:104–5

Reflect: Are there areas in your life that you're keeping in the dark? Why has it been difficult for you to bring them into the light of God's word?

2

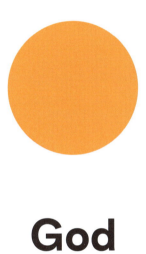

God

What We Believe

There is only one true God. He is unchanging, immense, eternal, and beyond human comprehension. He is almighty, most wise, and most holy. God is the source of all life and goodness in and of himself. He does not need anything that he made. He is most loving, gracious, merciful, and longsuffering—forgiving iniquity, transgression, and sin. He rewards those who diligently seek him. He hates sin and will not clear the guilty. In the unity of the Godhead there are three persons of one substance, power, and eternity: God the Father, God the Son, and God the Holy Spirit.

Why We Believe It

The passages below inform the Christian doctrine of God's existence and glory. God has spoken in the Bible, so we believe what he has said there. In the following pages, we'll explore this key doctrine and what it means for us as we follow Christ.

The LORD passed before him and proclaimed, "The LORD, the LORD, a God merciful and gracious, slow to anger, and abounding in steadfast love and faithfulness, keeping steadfast love for thousands, forgiving iniquity and transgression and sin, but who will by no means clear the guilty, visiting the iniquity of the fathers on the children and the children's children, to the third and the fourth generation."

Exodus 34:6–7

Who is a God like you, pardoning iniquity
   and passing over transgression
   for the remnant of his inheritance?
He does not retain his anger forever,
   because he delights in steadfast love.
He will again have compassion on us;
   he will tread our iniquities underfoot.
You will cast all our sins
   into the depths of the sea.
You will show faithfulness to Jacob
   and steadfast love to Abraham,
as you have sworn to our fathers
   from the days of old.

Micah 7:18–20

The LORD is a jealous and avenging God;
  the LORD is avenging and wrathful;
the LORD takes vengeance on his adversaries
  and keeps wrath for his enemies.
The LORD is slow to anger and great in power,
  and the LORD will by no means clear the guilty.
His way is in whirlwind and storm,
  and the clouds are the dust of his feet.

Nahum 1:2–3

And the Word became flesh and dwelt among us, and we have seen his glory, glory as of the only Son from the Father, full of grace and truth. (John bore witness about him, and cried out, "This was he of whom I said, 'He who comes after me ranks before me, because he was before me.'") For from his fullness we have all received, grace upon grace. For the law was given through Moses; grace and truth came through Jesus Christ. No one has ever seen God; the only God, who is at the Father's side, he has made him known.

John 1:14–18

Oh, the depth of the riches and wisdom and knowledge of God! How unsearchable are his judgments and how inscrutable his ways!

  "For who has known the mind of the Lord,
    or who has been his counselor?"
  "Or who has given a gift to him
    that he might be repaid?"

For from him and through him and to him are all things. To him be glory forever. Amen.

Romans 11:33–36

How It Matters

Throughout this chapter, we'll focus on the glory of God. There's no one else like him—he alone is God. He is breathtakingly powerful and beautiful, and he created everything in the universe to reflect his power and glory. God also created us to enjoy his power and glory. Sadly, because of sin, we often love the power and beauty of creation more than the Creator. Yet we cannot escape the reality of God; we live in his world. Through all its changes, ups, and downs, the unchanging God is faithful and dependable. And this God has revealed his glory most powerfully and beautifully in his Son. Jesus died to bring glorious grace and forgiveness to sinners. Now we can enjoy the glory of God once again!

1. How Big Is Your God?

I was raised in a Christian home. Yet as I was growing up, my thinking about God was far different from the picture of God found in the Bible. Then my brother Tedd came home from college and began to talk to me about God's total control over all things.

This was a piece of the doctrine of God I had never heard before. Our conversations flooded me with questions, hurt my pride, and made me angry. During one of our debates, I got so mad that I took off my shoe and threw it at Tedd. A day or so later, he brought me a paperback copy of the Bible and a yellow marker, and said, "This summer read through the Bible and mark every instance of the sovereign rule of God over all things."

I took the challenge. This summer reading project not only corrected my poor theology, it also changed the trajectory of my life. I was not only moved by the picture of God's complete rule, but I was also blown away by his immeasurable glory.

Few believers suffer from a view of God that's too big. Yet many suffer from a picture of God that is sadly too small. We can't allow ourselves to hold a theology that shrinks God down to a manageable size. Yet it's easy to do.

Here's the problem. When you are working to understand any concept or term, you always begin your process of understanding from the vantage point of your own experience. For example, if I use the term *father*, you will define that term based on your experience of your own father. Your understanding won't change until I define what I mean by that term.

Yet when it comes to God, no experience in my life is comparable to who and what he is. Our God is incomparable in the purity of his holiness and the expansiveness of his glory. For the rest of this chapter, I hope you'll see—and be blown away by—what God's word shows us of his brilliant glory.

Read: "O LORD, God of our fathers, are you not God in heaven? You rule over all the kingdoms of the nations. In your hand are power and might, so that none is able to withstand you." 2 CHRONICLES 20:6

Reflect: Have there been moments in your life when you felt awe or wonder at God's greatness?

---

2. The Glory War

God has no glory rival. There is only one who exists in the universe who is ultimate in glory, ultimate in greatness, ultimate in beauty, and ultimate in perfection. And because God is glorious, there's one thing you must understand: Life is one big glory war. Here's how the battle takes shape.

Each of us is hardwired by God for glory. We are attracted to glorious things, whether it's an exciting drama, an enthralling piece of music, or the best meal ever. God made us this way to drive us to him. We will always be shaped by the pursuit of some kind of glory. So the battle begins with this question: What glory right here, right now, has captured your heart?

Sin makes us all glory thieves. We take credit for what only God could produce. We want to be sovereign and we want to be worshiped. We complain when we don't get whatever it is that we want. But in living for our own glory, we steal glory that belongs to God.

Only God's glory can satisfy the glory hunger in our hearts. If you could experience the most glorious situations, locations, relationships, achievements, or possessions in life, your heart still would not be satisfied. Creation doesn't have the capacity to bring contentment to our hearts. That's not its purpose. Instead, creation is designed to point us to the glory of the one who can satiate our hunger and give peace and rest to our hearts.

God's grace alone has the power to win the glory war in our hearts. We all tend to continually revert back to self-glory. So the only hope for us is that the God of glory will rescue us from our glory thievery. In amazing grace, Jesus willingly came on a glory rescue mission. He lived righteously on our behalf, died for our thievery, and rose again, conquering sin and death. Because he did, there is hope that we will finally be free from self-glory and live forever in the light of the satisfying glory of God.

Read: "Yours, O LORD, is the greatness and the power and the glory and the victory and the majesty, for all that is in the heavens and in the earth is yours. Yours is the kingdom, O LORD, and you are exalted as head above all. Both riches and honor come from you, and you rule over all. In your hand are power and might, and in your hand it is to make great and to give strength to all. And now we thank you, our God, and praise your glorious name." 1 CHRONICLES 29:11–13

Reflect: Put the passage above on a card and tape it to the mirror you look in every morning.

---

3. A God-Shaped Life

Do you know the first four words of the Bible? Here they are: "In the beginning, God" (Gen. 1:1).

These may be not only the four most important words in the Bible but also the four most important words ever written. Why? Because the existence of God is so foundational, and because everyone lives in the context of how he or she thinks about God.

There is no place where the existence of God doesn't press upon and shape how you live. If you think (or deny) that God exists, that affects everything. Your view of God shapes the way you think about philosophy, science, psychology, politics, education, and entertainment. The way you approach your parents, your family members, your neighbors, your classmates, your teachers, your grandparents, your daily schoolwork, the joys and disappointments of life, your money, your body, your identity, your meaning and purpose, and your life and death are all somehow shaped by your view of God.

It is impossible for any human being anywhere to live in a way that does not reflect his or her view of God. God made us this way; it's wired into our humanity. And that means we should ask: Does my view of God reflect who he declares himself to be in his word?

Read: "Have you not known? Have you not heard? The LORD is the everlasting God, the Creator of the ends of the earth. He does not faint or grow weary; his understanding is unsearchable." ISAIAH 40:28

Reflect: Where do you see the reality of God shaping your life and your choices? How might that influence spread from just that one area to every other part of your life?

---

4. Do You Believe in God?

If you asked someone, "Does God exist?" you might expect a yes or a no. Either that person believes in God or doesn't. But the closer you get to where all of us live, these two categories seem inadequate. I want to broaden the categories for you.

First, there are people who deny God's existence.

As you grow up and go to school, you may be taught by brilliant and gifted teachers who know their subjects well but who don't believe in God. They may think we have evolved beyond any need for some ancient religion. Yet because they deny God, even these experts cannot give you an accurate view of the universe. And this means that it will be especially important for you to listen to biblical teaching from the Christians (perhaps parents and pastors) that God may have put in your life.

Second, there are people who admit there's a God but seem to have little desire to know him.

Sadly, there are millions of people in this category. They do not actually believe in God; what they believe in is the "god concept." These people tend not to have any kind of love for or worship of God. Their god is distant, impersonal, unattached, uninvolved, uncaring, inactive, powerless, and without authority. Whatever concept they have of God is distant from anything Scripture describes him to be.

Third, there are people who are practical atheists.

For these people, there is nothing more important, more central, more heart engaging, and more formative than their belief in God and their relationship with their Savior and Lord. They love God with all their hearts—but not always.

As long as sin still lives inside of us, every true believer fits into this category of practical atheism. No, I'm not talking about rejecting the existence of God. Instead, there are moments when we think, desire, speak, or act as if God doesn't exist.

Here are some examples. Perhaps it's a moment when we cheat on an exam or indulge in gossip. Maybe it's a moment when we give way to lust or make ourselves the center of attention by taking too much credit. Maybe it's buying something that we do not need. Perhaps it's a moment when we decide the acceptance of our friends is more important than obeying our parents.

So when God—by his grace—convicts our hearts and reveals our practical atheism, it's important that we have hearts ready to confess our sin to him. We all need to cry out for his protecting, rescuing, and enabling grace.

Read: "And without faith it is impossible to please him, for whoever would draw near to God must believe that he exists and that he rewards those who seek him." HEBREWS 11:6

Reflect: Where are you susceptible to act, react, or respond as if God doesn't exist?

---

5. Seeing the Glory of God

The created world is jam-packed with glory. God designed the physical world to reveal his character. All creation together is one big finger pointing to God. This reality spans every period of human history, every location on the globe, and every racial and ethnic group.

You see God's glory in the sand dunes in Dubai and in the lush green valleys of New Zealand. You see it in the frozen tundra of the polar regions and the dense jungles of the Amazon. You see it in the inexhaustible wings of a hummingbird and the lumbering gait of an elephant. You see his glory in the bright rays of the sun and in the twinkling starry night. You see it in the multitude of faces on the streets of New York and in a pride of lions in the bush of Africa. You hear it in the rhythm of ocean waves and in the whisper of the wind through the trees. You see his glory when water boils and smell it in well-roasted beef. You see it in the passing of the seasons and in the regularity of morning and night. Fish, fowl, and flowers constantly point to him. Your local park, your favorite pet, and the garden out back are all fingers pointing to him. It is a 24/7 glory display for everyone to see, no ticket needed.

There is a calling for all of us in this. Talk with your neighbor about the God behind the roses and the sunset. Tell your friends that every time you go to the park and walk through the woods, you think about the one who created it all. Do everything you can to give spiritually blind people eyes to see, and pray that as they begin to see God, they will seek him.

Humbly thank him for the grace of this daily display. Pray for eyes that are open to his glory and a heart that remembers. Determine that you won't pick a flower, boil an egg, look out the window, pet the dog, or mash some potatoes without a moment of worship, and then ask for grace to follow through.

Read: "The heavens declare the glory of God, and the sky above proclaims his handiwork." PSALM 19:1

Reflect: What part of creation has had your attention recently? What do you love about it? How can that creation beauty point you to the Creator?

---

6. Unchanging God

As parents, Luella and I dealt with a frustration that all parents experience. Just about when we felt comfortable parenting our children through a particular stage of development, they would move on to another stage. Nothing stays the same.

Our bodies are in an ongoing state of change. Our emotions swing widely and change constantly. Physical things age, wear out, and break. The fact that people change all the time often makes our relationships confusing and difficult. Culture and technology are changing so rapidly it's nearly impossible to keep up. And as we go through the stages of life, our daily opportunities, responsibilities, and temptations morph and change.

Because of all this change, we all seek for some rock of stability in life. We all would love to hook ourselves to something that we could be sure would stay the same no matter what.

This kind of reliability is found only in our God, who does not change. He is what he has always been, and he always will be what he forever has been. So God never becomes something, never needs anything, and never learns anything. He will never grow into something different than he once was. God will only ever be what he eternally is.

There is no better to-the-point summary of this than Malachi 3:6: "For I the LORD do not change; therefore you, O children of Jacob, are not consumed." If our relationship with God rested on whether or not *we* were unchangingly faithful, we would be doomed. Thankfully, our fickle hearts don't alter his loving purpose.

"I the LORD do not change" is what gives you the courage to stand for Christ at school, even when you're misunderstood or mocked. It is why you dig into God's word, even on the mornings when you're tired and facing a full schedule. It's what propels you to love that friend who seems to be looking for a fight. It is what causes you to run to God and not away from him when faced with temptations. And it is what gives you a reason to come to him in humble confession when you have wandered away from his will.

"I the LORD do not change" is the rock on which your life as a Christian rests. Live in this unchanging hope.

Read: "Of old you laid the foundation of the earth, and the heavens are the work of your hands. They will perish, but you will remain; they will all wear out like a garment. You will change them like a robe, and they will pass away, but you are the same, and your years have no end." PSALM 102:25–27

Reflect: Since people are unpredictable, helping them can sometimes be demanding and discouraging. How can God's unchanging nature give you strength and hope to keep being a tool of grace in their lives?

7. Time for a Tune Up

A world-class orchestra doesn't begin a concert by launching into a symphony without any preparation. No, the musicians begin by tuning their various instrument groups until each player is ready to perform in harmony with every other player. Similarly, it's vital to tune your heart to live in harmony with your Maker.

Tuning our hearts requires time and effort. But it is spiritually rewarding and energizing. Let me suggest what it looks like to tune your heart to live in harmony with God.

Gaze. Take a few moments each morning to go to one of those wonderful passages in Scripture that displays for you God's glory (Ps. 27). It's like a good painting; each time you look, you see something more fully, you see something different, or you see the whole as you never have seen it before.

Search. You need time not just to read your Bible but also to unpack it, tear it apart, and reflect over and over on what you've read. Yet it is not enough to come to know the word of God; the goal of all Bible study is to come to know, love, worship, and serve the God of the word. Your Bible is a narrative of his glory. Start every day by finding him in his story.

Worship. Begin every day by bowing in adoration and awe before the great "I am." Speak to him in praise for who he is and in gratitude for what he has done. Defeat the idols of your heart every morning with adoration of the one who alone is worthy of your worship.

Surrender. Each morning consciously surrender to the Lord the ownership of your personality, your mentality, your emotionality, your spirituality, your physicality, and your sexuality. Place your whole life on his altar for his using.

Confess. Start every morning by coming out of hiding, lifting off your shoulders the burden of sin that you carry, casting your burden on the Lord, and then basking in his forgiving and restoring grace.

Celebrate. Rather than starting your day by grumbling about what the next few hours may bring, start by jumping for joy! Why? Because the King of kings has welcomed you into his family forever.

Repeat. I am afraid many of us make spiritual commitments that end up not having a long shelf life. Determine to nail the tuning of your heart into your morning schedule. Then pray for the enabling grace to follow through for the long run.

Read: "Hear, O LORD, when I cry aloud; be gracious to me and answer me! You have said, 'Seek my face.' My heart says to you, 'Your face, LORD, do I seek.'" PSALM 27:7–8

Reflect: Ask the Lord to make the tuning of your heart to his glory a long-term habit of your life.

3

God's Holiness

What We Believe

There is only one living and true God. He is infinite in being and perfection, a most pure spirit. God is holy in all his purposes, all his works, and all his commands. He is due whatever worship, service, and obedience he is pleased to require from angels, people, and every other creature.

Why We Believe It

The passages below inform the Christian doctrine of God's holiness. God has spoken in the Bible, so we believe what he has said there. In the following pages, we'll explore this key doctrine and what it means for us as we follow Christ.

There is none holy like the LORD:
 for there is none besides you;
 there is no rock like our God.

1 Samuel 2:2

In the year that King Uzziah died I saw the Lord sitting upon a throne, high and lifted up; and the train of his robe filled the temple. Above him stood the seraphim. Each had six wings: with two he covered his face, and with two he covered his feet, and with two he flew. And one called to another and said:

 "Holy, holy, holy is the LORD of hosts;
 the whole earth is full of his glory!"

And the foundations of the thresholds shook at the voice of him who called, and the house was filled with smoke. And I said: "Woe is me! For I am lost; for I am a man of unclean lips, and I dwell in the midst of a people of unclean lips; for my eyes have seen the King, the LORD of hosts!"

Then one of the seraphim flew to me, having in his hand a burning coal that he had taken with tongs from the altar. And he touched my mouth and said: "Behold, this has touched your lips; your guilt is taken away, and your sin atoned for."

Isaiah 6:1–7

For thus says the One who is high and lifted up,
 who inhabits eternity, whose name is Holy:
"I dwell in the high and holy place,
 and also with him who is of a contrite and lowly spirit,
to revive the spirit of the lowly,
 and to revive the heart of the contrite."

Isaiah 57:15

As he who called you is holy, you also be holy in all your conduct, since it is written, "You shall be holy, for I am holy."

1 Peter 1:15–16

And the four living creatures, each of them with six wings, are full of eyes all around and within, and day and night they never cease to say,

 "Holy, holy, holy, is the Lord God Almighty,
 who was and is and is to come!"

Revelation 4:8

How It Matters

Throughout this chapter, we'll focus on God's holiness. God himself is holy—that is, he is absolutely unique, far greater and different than anything else. He alone is God. When we get a glimpse of God's holiness, it stretches our imagination. For his holiness isn't just one part of who he is; God is completely holy—through and through. And so is his every action, word, and plan. So if you don't understand God's holiness, you won't understand God or life. But a biblical view of our holy God will help you truly see both your sin and God's grace. His holiness will both open your heart to serve him in the world and also open your eyes to see him in his word.

1. What Is Holiness?

Everywhere you go in Dubai, you are confronted with the Burj Khalifa, the world's tallest building. Impressive skyscrapers are all around Dubai, but the Burj Khalifa looms over them all with majestic glory.

On a swelteringly hot Dubai morning, I got out of a car near the Burj Khalifa and began to walk toward this magnificent feat of architecture. Even from far away, it was hard to crane my head back far enough to see all the way to the top. The closer I got, the more imposing and amazing this structure became. As I walked, there was no thought of the other buildings in Dubai that had previously impressed me. As amazing as those buildings were, they were simply not comparable in stunning architectural grandeur and perfection to this one.

When I finally got to the base of the Burj Khalifa, I felt incredibly small, like an ant at the base of a light pole. I entered a futuristic looking elevator and, in what seemed like seconds, was on the 125th floor.

GOD'S HOLINESS 31

This was not the top of the building—that was closed to visitors. As I stepped to the windows to get a feel for how high I was and to scan the city of Dubai, I immediately commented on how small the rest of the buildings looked. Those "small" buildings were skyscrapers. I had experienced the greatest, and that put what had impressed me before into a different perspective.

Similarly, holiness marks something as being in a class of its own, distinct from anything else. God is holy; he is unique. There is no comparing anything to him. The Bible's word for *holiness* comes from a Hebrew word that means "to cut." To be holy means to be cut off, or separate, from everything else. You can't say God is like something because there is nothing in all the universe that he is like.

My prayer for me and for you is that when it comes to God's holiness, our perspective will be like mine was that morning in Dubai, standing at the base of the Burj Khalifa, and then looking down from its heights at everything else. There is no holiness as holy as God's holiness.

Read: "To whom then will you compare me, that I should be like him? says the Holy One." ISAIAH 40:25

Reflect: What are some steps you can take to see the grandeur and magnificence of God's holiness even better?

---

2. Imagine This!

All children have a powerful capacity to imagine. It makes the world of a child surprising, delightful, captivating, and wonderful. My granddaughter demonstrates this ability every time we are together. She carefully makes me tea and a sandwich, but the cup is actually empty and the plate holds no food. Yet she can see both, and she's delighted when I tell her what a wonderful cook she is.

When it comes to faith, *imagination is not the ability to conjure up what is unreal but the capacity to perceive what is real but unseen.* What happens when your religious system centers on surrendering to a God you cannot see, touch, or hear? Imagination is important.

To enable this, God has given you a dual sight system. You see physical things with your eyes, but you also have the eyes of the heart to see unseen spiritual realities. The problem is that sin renders us spiritually blind. So God blesses us with the sight-giving ministry of the Holy

Spirit. With his help, we can "see" what cannot be seen with the physical eye but is real.

The prophet Isaiah, at his calling, also saw what he had not seen before. He received a vision of the Lord sitting on his throne. And he heard angels making this declaration: "Holy, holy, holy is the LORD of hosts; the whole earth is full of his glory!" (Isa. 6:3).

It wasn't enough for the angels to say "God is holy." No, the angels had to say *holy* three times to capture the depth and breadth of God's holiness. It's as if I were to say to you, "I saw this guy at the ball game who was huge, huge, huge!" You would know right away that this was not an average big guy. You would know that this guy was the biggest guy I had ever seen.

"Holy, holy, holy" is meant to stretch the boundaries of your imagination.

Would you stop and pray that the eyes of your heart would open? Ask God to give you even a little glimpse of the mind-blowing grandeur of his holiness. Why? Seeing his holiness will change you and the way you live forever.

Read: "Holy, holy, holy is the LORD of hosts; the whole earth is full of his glory!" ISAIAH 6:3

Reflect: When was the last time you were blown away by the grandeur of God? What happened that led you to see his glory and holiness?

---

3. Wholly Holy

God's holiness is not an *aspect* of what he is. No, God's holiness is the *essence* of what he is.

If you were to ask, "How is the holiness of God revealed?" the only right answer is "In everything he does."

Everything God thinks, desires, speaks, and does is utterly holy in every way. He is holy in every attribute and every action.

He is holy in justice.

He is holy in love.

He is holy in mercy.

He is holy in power.

He is holy in sovereignty.

He is holy in wisdom.

He is holy in patience.

He is holy in anger.

He is holy in grace.

He is holy in faithfulness.

He is holy in compassion.

He is even holy in his holiness; it's what he is.

Not only that, holiness sits at the center of the grand narrative of the gospel of Jesus Christ.

Without the holiness of God, there would be no moral law to which every human being is responsible.

Without the holiness of God, there would be no divine anger over sin.

Without the holiness of God, there would be no perfect Son sent as an acceptable sacrifice for sin.

Without the holiness of God, there would have been no vindication of the resurrection.

Without the holiness of God, there would be no final defeat of sin and Satan.

Without the holiness of God, there would be no hope of a new heaven and earth where holiness will reign over us and in us forever.

The biblical story would not be the biblical story if it were not written and controlled at every point by one who is holy all the time and in every way.

God reveals his holiness to us not as a warning that we should run from him in eternal terror. Instead, the Holy One extends a welcome to us so that we would run to him. Only there may weak and failing sinners always find grace that lasts forever.

Read: "Exalt the LORD our God; worship at his footstool! Holy is he!" PSALM 99:5

Reflect: Does God's holiness make you want to run toward him or away from him? Why? How does the good news of what Jesus has done for you change your perspective?

---

4. The Key to Understanding Life

Have you ever heard politicians, educators, social media influencers, or entertainment icons talk about holiness? It has no purpose or meaning for them.

Holiness doesn't enter into our concept of success. Holiness never is discussed when people are talking about plans for their summers. Holiness is viewed as a dusty religious concept with little practical meaning.

But without the holiness of God, life will always be puzzling.

God intends his holiness to be at the center of how you make sense of life. The holiness of God must be at the center of what you have concluded to be true. If it's not, you will never understand the universe properly. And you won't live the way you were designed to live.

> In the year that King Uzziah died I saw the Lord sitting upon a throne, high and lifted up; and the train of his robe filled the temple. Above him stood the seraphim. Each had six wings: with two he covered his face, and with two he covered his feet, and with two he flew. And one called to another and said:
>
> "Holy, holy, holy is the LORD of hosts;
> the whole earth is full of his glory!" (Isa. 6:1–3)

In this amazing scene, we learn that God is so holy that the entire earth is filled to the brim with the incomparable glory of his holiness. Without this, it is impossible to understand anything in your life correctly.

Every good thing ever created has existed because the Holy One sits on the throne of the universe all the time. Your sense of identity and purpose; how you use your energy, time, and money; your sense of right and wrong; your means of making decisions; and where you look for peace and rest must be connected to this declaration: "Holy, holy, holy is the LORD of hosts; the whole earth is full of his glory!"

God's holiness is the key to understanding life. It's your light in darkness, your GPS when you feel lost, your comfort in the face of the evils of this fallen world, the constant reminder of who you are and what you need, and the place you run when everywhere else has proven inadequate.

Read: "I am the LORD, your Holy One, the Creator of Israel, your King."
ISAIAH 43:15

Reflect: When was the last time you paused from the busyness of life to think about God's holiness? How did his holiness affect you?

5. Holy, Holy, Holy

God's holiness is intensely and expansively practical. It changes the way you understand everything. And because it does, it changes the way you live with and relate to everything.

The holiness of God confronts us with the sinfulness of sin (Isa. 6:5). Sin doesn't always seem sinful to us. It often looks more beautiful and pleasurable than dangerous and destructive. If you're eating a third piece of chocolate cake in a moment of gluttony, at the moment you are experiencing not destruction and danger but the taste of deep, rich chocolate wrapped in silky buttercream. Yet every time I sin, I turn my back on God's holy rule.

So what do we do with this? We must cry out for eyes to see and a heart to weep. Then we will find the joy of discovering mercies that are new once again.

The holiness of God is the reason we'll never outgrow God's grace (Isa. 6:6-7). In the throne room scene of Isaiah 6, the glory of God's holiness meets the ugliness of sin. Yet this meeting displays that you and I will never outgrow God's grace and forgiveness. The longer you live in the presence of God's holiness, the more you become aware of the depth and extent of your sin, the more you are dependent on God's grace, and the more you are amazed by his patience.

The glory of God's holiness propels us to give ourselves to his mission of redeeming grace (Isa. 6:8-9). When faced with the glory of God's holiness and the disaster of his own sin, Isaiah responded not only with confession but also with willingness to give himself to God's mission: " 'Here I am! Send me.' And he said, 'Go.' "

Many of us don't share Isaiah's willingness. We view our lives as belonging to us. We're willing to give God only occasional portions. I'm not talking here about being a pastor or missionary. Yet each of us is called to be on God's mission, no matter what he has gifted and called us to do.

Read: "Who is like you, O LORD, among the gods? Who is like you, majestic in holiness, awesome in glorious deeds, doing wonders?" EXODUS 15:11

Reflect: As you think about the situations and locations of your life, what would it look like to live every day in constant recognition of the holiness of God?

6. True Meaning and Purpose

God intends the messiness of life to be transformative.

Each area is meant to prepare you for what is to come—that is, to be a tool of an increasing spiritual hunger and growth. God uses all of the difficulties of life in this fallen world to accomplish the most important thing that could ever be accomplished for you and in you. It is God's goal that you would progressively become holy as he is holy.

As this happens, you become more and more ready for your heavenly life, where holiness is the eternal norm. Here is where ultimate meaning and purpose are found. God uses even the hardest things to produce the most wonderful of things.

Through it all, you can be assured that you are being prepared. And at the heart of that preparation is this purpose: that you would progressively become holy as he is holy. This process gives meaning to all of life.

Ultimate meaning is found in God's holiness. Human meaning is rooted in the existence and plan of a God who is gloriously holy in every way. Your Lord would never plan, rule, and direct your life in a way that is anything less than perfectly holy.

Now, that should give you reason for rest and celebration.

Read: "Who will not fear, O Lord, and glorify your name? For you alone are holy. All nations will come and worship you, for your righteous acts have been revealed." REVELATION 15:4

Reflect: Where are you tempted to doubt that God has designed holy and good purposes for your life?

7. The Purpose of All Biblical and Theological Study

The ultimate reason humans have the ability to think and communicate is this: so we can know God and commune with him. Consider what God's word promises in Isaiah 55:

> For as the rain and the snow come down from heaven
>   and do not return there but water the earth,
> making it bring forth and sprout,
>   giving seed to the sower and bread to the eater,
> so shall my word be that goes out from my mouth;
>   it shall not return to me empty,
> but it shall accomplish that which I purpose,
>   and shall succeed in the thing for which I sent it. . . .
> Instead of the thorn shall come up the cypress;
>   instead of the brier shall come up the myrtle;
> and it shall make a name for the LORD,
>   an everlasting sign that shall not be cut off." (Isa. 55:10–11, 13)

What is the promise? It's that the word of God, empowered by the Spirit of God and received by the people of God, will always accomplish its purpose.

When God says to you, "My word will always accomplish its purpose," your question should immediately be "What is the purpose of God's word?"

This question gets at the heart of God's purpose for all biblical and theological study, whether at the highest level of scholarship in an academic setting or in the average person's daily Bible study. Why study God's word? Why study theology? What should result from our study?

The purpose of the word of God is deeper than the dissemination of biblical and theological information. The goal is radical heart and life transformation.

God intends the information to be transformative. Biblical literacy and theological knowledge were never meant to be ends in themselves, but rather means to an end. The end is personal holiness.

Read: "Sanctify them in the truth; your word is truth." JOHN 17:17

Reflect: What's your main goal for the time you spend reading and studying God's word?

4

God's Sovereignty

What We Believe

God, the Creator of all things, has wisely and freely ordained everything that comes to pass. He also upholds, directs, and governs all creatures, actions, and things, from the greatest to the least. Yet God isn't the author of sin, and he doesn't violate the will of his creatures. In his ordinary providence, God makes use of means. Yet he is free to work without, above, and against them at his pleasure. In the end, everything that happens will result in the praise of the glory of his wisdom, power, justice, goodness, and mercy.

Why We Believe It

The passages below inform the Christian doctrine of God's sovereignty. God has spoken in the Bible, so we believe what he has said there. In the following pages, we'll explore this key doctrine and what it means for us as we follow Christ.

Whatever the Lord pleases, he does,
in heaven and on earth,
in the seas and all deeps.

Psalm 135:6

Declaring the end from the beginning
and from ancient times things not yet done,
saying, "My counsel shall stand,
and I will accomplish all my purpose,"
calling a bird of prey from the east,
the man of my counsel from a far country.
I have spoken, and I will bring it to pass;
I have purposed, and I will do it.

Isaiah 46:10–11

At the end of the days I, Nebuchadnezzar, lifted my eyes to heaven, and my reason returned to me, and I blessed the Most High, and praised and honored him who lives forever,

for his dominion is an everlasting dominion,
    and his kingdom endures from generation to generation;
all the inhabitants of the earth are accounted as nothing,
    and he does according to his will among the host of heaven
    and among the inhabitants of the earth;
and none can stay his hand
    or say to him, "What have you done?"

Daniel 4:34–35

Blessed be the God and Father of our Lord Jesus Christ, who has blessed us in Christ with every spiritual blessing in the heavenly places, even as he chose us in him before the foundation of the world, that we should be holy and blameless before him. In love he predestined us for adoption to himself as sons through Jesus Christ, according to the purpose of his will, to the praise of his glorious grace, with which he has blessed us in the Beloved. In him we have redemption through his blood, the forgiveness of our trespasses, according to the riches of his grace, which he lavished upon us, in all wisdom and insight making known to us the mystery of his will, according to his purpose, which he set forth in Christ as a plan for the fullness of time, to unite all things in him, things in heaven and things on earth.

In him we have obtained an inheritance, having been predestined according to the purpose of him who works all things according to the counsel of his will, so that we who were the first to hope in Christ might be to the praise of his glory. In him you also, when you heard the word of truth, the gospel of your salvation, and believed in him, were sealed with the promised Holy Spirit, who is the guarantee of our inheritance until we acquire possession of it, to the praise of his glory.

Ephesians 1:3–14

How It Matters

Throughout this chapter, we'll focus on the sovereignty of God. The Lord is in charge of every thing, every person, and every situation. He is God. And everything he plans (decrees) happens according to his plan (providence). Nothing is ever out of his control. Yet all of us want to be in charge—little sovereigns over our lives. However, we don't have control. So God wants us to trust him and to humble ourselves under his sovereign wisdom. Even though there's a lot we don't understand about what God is doing, we can trust him because the one who's in control of all things is also our Father.

1. He Is God; I Am Not

I have endured much physical sickness and suffering in the last several years. I am doing well now, yet I will deal with sickness and a weakened body until I die. Thankfully, the most severe moments of my suffering were marked with a deep joy. No, I wasn't celebrating my pain. But in those moments, I was crying out to one who was sovereign over every element of what I was experiencing.

When I cried, "Lord, help me; Lord, help me," I knew that my sovereign Father heard me. I knew he had both the willingness and the power to answer. I trust I will not have to endure that pain again. However, I am thankful that those moments were infused with that joy. Here's why: I knew that my Father is King of kings and Lord of lords.

Here's the big issue in these moments: What do you do when you are weary and distraught? What do you do when your heart seems like it can't carry any more? In these moments, where do you run?

As I read the Bible, I am reminded that no matter how things look at street level, God is Lord over every situation that confuses and distresses me.

No, the pain of life in this sin-shattered world won't fade away. Yes, I will face dark moments again. Yet I can be free from panic because there is one who is in control. And he is perfectly wise and good.

So I can rest in knowing that what I don't understand, he perfectly plans. I can find peace in knowing that what I could never rule, he rules. In both hard times and easy times, it is glorious to know that God rules and we don't.

Read: "Behold, I am the Lord, the God of all flesh. Is anything too hard for me?" JEREMIAH 32:27

Reflect: In what areas are you hesitant or maybe even scared to trust the Lord's control of your life? Why?

---

2. But Why?

"Why?" is a question we ask all our lives. Toddlers love to ask this question as they try to understand the world around them. But even in old age we ask, "Why are things the way they are? Why can't I . . . ? Why would God allow . . . ?"

"Why?" is one of the most profound and practical questions a person can consider. Are we and our world under any control? Is God sovereign? The Bible answers, "Yes."

So what does it mean that the Bible teaches that God is sovereign? It means that God alone determines all that will happen and rules how everything will happen. This means that he never is surprised, never is frustrated, never wonders, never looks back with regret, never is waiting, and never feels helpless.

God is never forced to do something. There is no authority over him that he has to answer to. He does what he pleases, decides whatever he wants, and acts as he desires. To say God is sovereign is simply to say that he is God and there is no one like him.

There are two aspects of God's sovereignty: his decrees and his providence.

God's decrees. A decree is a decision made by an authority. According to his own will and for his own glory, God has decided everything that will come to pass. Because he is infinite in power and wisdom, his decrees are eternal and unchangeable. What God has decreed to happen will happen.

God's providence. Yet God doesn't just give a decree and then sit passively above his world. He is an active participant in his world. He governs, sustains, effects, and controls. God is in constant contact with the universe, governing everything—from the biggest things all the way down to the smallest things.

God is sovereign. He decrees what will be and rules what he has made. How encouraging to know that our world is not out of control! No matter how chaotic and confusing it may seem, everything in your life is under the wise and careful control of the Lord Almighty.

Read: "God is not man, that he should lie, or a son of man, that he should change his mind. Has he said, and will he not do it? Or has he spoken, and will he not fulfill it?" NUMBERS 23:19

Reflect: Where are you tempted to think that God is actually not in control?

---

3. Out of Control!

Much of our regular anxiety, fear, and discouragement comes from thinking things are out of control. But what we're really struggling with is this: Things are out of *our* control.

Imagine I have placed a sheet of paper in front of you with a small circle inside of a much larger circle. We'll call the inner circle *the circle of responsibility* and the outer circle *the circle of concern.* Living as God has called you to live requires knowing which things in your life fit into which circle.

The circle of responsibility represents things that God has called you to do. These are your daily, God-ordained duties. The only proper response to this inner circle is to carefully and faithfully obey while trusting God for his empowering grace.

Many other things in life grab your attention, capture your mind, and weigh heavily on your heart—but they're not your responsibility. These things don't fit in the inner circle. Instead, they fit in the outer circle, the circle of concern. The only proper way to respond to these concerns is to entrust them to your Lord, who governs them all for his glory and your ultimate good.

What happens if you load things into the inner circle that actually belong to God? You will be domineering and controlling, and your life will be marked by anxiety and fear.

God hasn't just given us a set of responsibilities (the inner circle). He has also pulled back the curtain of the heavens to reveal to us his sovereign throne (the outer circle). He has done this for two reasons. First, he wants us to be good stewards of the few things he has placed under our control. Second, he wants us to rest in knowing that the things that are out of our control are under his sovereign control.

The questions for you are "Do you have a clear understanding in your life of the things that God has called you to do (the inner circle)?" and "Do you understand which things he welcomes you to entrust to him (the outer circle)?"

Read: "Are not two sparrows sold for a penny? And not one of them will fall to the ground apart from your Father. But even the hairs of your head are all numbered. Fear not, therefore; you are of more value than many sparrows." MATTHEW 10:29–31

Reflect: Think of how different your attitude and emotions would be if you really believed that there's never a situation, location, or relationship in your life that isn't ruled by King Christ.

---

4. We All Want to Be Sovereign

Why do drivers get angry at the cars in front of them? Why are vacations sometimes disappointing and not as fun as we had hoped? Why do we hate waiting in line at the grocery store? And why are we not always patient with family members or friends?

Deep in our hearts, we desire the world to follow our sovereign plans! We want the people around us to do our bidding! So we get easily frustrated because we lack the power to make things work the way we wish they would work.

It's been this way for a long time. In Genesis 3, Adam and Eve wanted a life that did not require them to obey their Creator. The horrible lie of the serpent was that human sovereignty was possible. We want to rule over things that we have no ability to rule. As God's sovereign will is happening around us, we get mad. Why? Because we would rather have our will be done.

Where does the desire to be sovereign rear its ugly head in your life? Every one of us would benefit from making this a daily item for personal prayer, saying,

Father, I confess that I often desire to have the rule over people and things that are under your control. May you give me the grace today to resist those desires and to entrust my life to you. I confess my sin against you and others, and I rest in your forgiveness.

Then leave your time of prayer thankful that you are free of the burden of sovereignty.

Read: "Let the heavens be glad, and let the earth rejoice, and let them say among the nations, 'The LORD reigns!'" 1 CHRONICLES 16:31

Reflect: Take a moment to praise God—because the one who sits on the throne and cares for you is your good Father.

---

5. Humble Hearts and Huge Harvests

It is humbling to stop and realize the limits of our sovereignty. Be honest: there are very few things we can control. I have a hard time controlling my car keys, my cell phone, and my earbuds.

This means that the doctrine of the sovereignty of God should humble us. Consider what James says about this:

Come now, you who say, "Today or tomorrow we will go into such and such a town and spend a year there and trade and make a profit"—yet you do not know what tomorrow will bring. What is your life? For you are a mist that appears for a little time and then vanishes. Instead you ought to say, "If the Lord wills, we will live and do this or that." (James 4:13–15)

It is tempting to act as if we are in more control than we actually are.

It is tempting to take credit for things we could have never produced on our own.

It is tempting to think that we can make life work according to our plan.

It is tempting to be proud of ourselves in places where we should instead be praising God.

The fact is, we have no idea what tomorrow will bring because we don't plan or control tomorrow; God alone does.

Here is the point: The sovereignty of God is deeply humbling. And this is good because:

A humble heart is a worshiping heart.

A humble heart is a grateful heart.

A humble heart is an obedient heart.

A humble heart is a loving, serving heart.

The sovereignty of God, carried in your heart, will produce a harvest of good fruit in your life.

Read: "I form light and create darkness; I make well-being and create calamity; I am the LORD, who does all these things. . . . Woe to him who strives with him who formed him, a pot among earthen pots! Does the clay say to him who forms it, 'What are you making?' or 'Your work has no handles'?" ISAIAH 45:7, 9

Reflect: Where do you tend to think that you have life under some kind of control? How do you respond when that area feels out of control? Why?

---

6. Unsolved Mysteries

We don't like to be confused. We don't like to be surprised. And we don't like to live with unsolved mysteries. Yet there are things that we will never fully understand. This has been the problem of believers of every generation.

- Did the world of Egypt seem under God's control to the Israelite slaves?
- Did things seem to be under God's control when Israel was ruled by wicked kings?
- Did it look like God was in control when Rome ruled Israel with a heavy hand?
- Did it appear that God was on the throne when Jerusalem and the temple were destroyed?
- Does it look like God is in control when the forces of nature run wild, killing thousands?

- Does it seem like God is in control when you seek to follow him and experience suffering while your non-Christian friend seems to have the good life?

When our children were young, they had little understanding of life and its dangers. So at times I'd have to say no to them, even when I knew they wouldn't be able to understand the reason. They'd be upset and ask, "Daddy, why? *Why?*"

And I would say, "Daddy would love to help you to understand why. But if I told you why, you still wouldn't understand. Does your daddy love you? Does he want good things for you? Does he want to keep you safe? Then trust your daddy. Walk down the hall and say to yourself, 'I don't know why my daddy said no to me, but I know my daddy loves me.'"

Rest is first found not in understanding things but in trusting your heavenly Father. He's the one who lovingly and wisely rules all the things you wish you could figure out.

So walk down the hallway of your life today and say, "There are many things I don't understand, but I know my Father is in control. I know he is wise and good, and I know he loves me."

You can rest with confidence in God's sovereignty precisely because God, in his word, has clearly and repeatedly said he is sovereign. Ultimately, rest is found not in knowing but in trusting.

Read: "Therefore do not be anxious, saying, 'What shall we eat?' or 'What shall we drink?' or 'What shall we wear?' For the Gentiles seek after all these things, and your heavenly Father knows that you need them all. But seek first the kingdom of God and his righteousness, and all these things will be added to you." MATTHEW 6:31-33

Reflect: Which of the listed items above is most difficult for you to understand? Why? Take a moment to tell your Father all about it.

7. "All Things Work Out for Good?"

All too often, I have heard people quote Romans 8:28 to those who are suffering: "And we know that for those who love God all things work together for good, for those who are called according to his purpose."

Many Christians take this passage to mean that hard things in their lives will eventually have a happy ending. Well-meaning Christians often say to those who are struggling, "Don't give up, all things work together for good."

I call this a *happy endings theology*. And it has infected the church.

If you read the next two verses of Romans 8, you'll see what Paul actually wants his readers to understand. Nothing they are facing has the ability to stop the march of God's redemptive plan or can separate them from his love:

> For those whom he foreknew he also predestined to be conformed to the image of his Son, in order that he might be the firstborn among many brothers. And those whom he predestined he also called, and those whom he called he also justified, and those whom he justified he also glorified. (Rom. 8:29–30)

These verses explain the "good" that is being promised in verse 28. It is not a promise of a happy family, a good marriage, a successful career, a wonderful church, physical health, or a comfortable life.

It is not situational good.

It is not relational good.

It is not financial good.

It is not locational good.

Instead, the good that is promised here is the most wonderful kind. It is the good of God's rescuing, forgiving, transforming, and delivering grace.

Yes, God does promise to exercise his sovereign authority and power for your good. He does bring good things out of bad things, but not happy endings. Instead, he promises the good of his unrelenting grace.

You can celebrate God's sovereignty not because it guarantees you a happy and comfortable life. Instead, his sovereign control connects you to him and the wonder of his inseparable love and unstoppable grace.

Read: "And after you have suffered a little while, the God of all grace, who has called you to his eternal glory in Christ, will himself restore, confirm, strengthen, and establish you. To him be the dominion forever and ever. Amen." 1 PETER 5:10-11

Reflect: What kind of good do you most often think God has in store for you? How is God helping you see differently when it comes to how you view his good for your life?

5

God's Power

What We Believe

God is omnipotent, almighty in power. He can do, without effort, whatever he wills at any time and in any place he chooses to exercise his power. This is the highest possible definition of power. It means God is utterly and completely unique in power. There is nothing in heaven or on earth like his power—it has no limits. There is nothing that God cannot do, according to his holy will and pleasure. And nothing can limit or stop God's exercise of his power.

Why We Believe It

The passages below inform the Christian doctrine of God's power. God has spoken in the Bible, so we believe what he has said there. In the following pages, we'll explore this key doctrine and what it means for us as we follow Christ.

And the LORD said to Moses, "Is the LORD's hand shortened? Now you shall see whether my word will come true for you or not."

Numbers 11:23

Thus says the LORD, the King of Israel
    and his Redeemer, the LORD of hosts:
"I am the first and I am the last;
    besides me there is no god.
Who is like me? Let him proclaim it.
    Let him declare and set it before me,
since I appointed an ancient people.
    Let them declare what is to come, and what will happen.
Fear not, nor be afraid;
    have I not told you from of old and declared it?
    And you are my witnesses!
Is there a God besides me?
    There is no Rock; I know not any."

Isaiah 44:6–8

Ah, Lord GOD! It is you who have made the heavens and the earth by your great power and by your outstretched arm! Nothing is too hard for you.

Jeremiah 32:17

And when he got into the boat, his disciples followed him. And behold, there arose a great storm on the sea, so that the boat was being swamped by the waves; but he was asleep. And they went and woke him, saying, "Save us, Lord; we are perishing." And he said to them, "Why are you afraid, O you of little faith?" Then he rose and rebuked the winds and the sea, and there was a great calm. And the men marveled, saying, "What sort of man is this, that even winds and sea obey him?"

Matthew 8:23–27

How It Matters

 Throughout this chapter, we'll focus on the power of God. He is almighty—more powerful than anything else. No other power can compare with God's might. He can create something out of nothing. He can bring life out of death. He gives strength to the weak and undeserving. And he helps his children do what seems impossible—to obey and follow him, and to love and forgive others. The reality is that since God is powerful, Christians must admit our weakness. On our own, we are not enough. But the good news is that the almighty one, who gives power to the weak, is also our Father. He is not only able to give us strength, but also loves to help his children.

1. Behold the Almighty!

I have a son who is a sports broadcaster. One Saturday afternoon, he texted me. He told me to turn on one of the sports channels because something amazing was happening. What I witnessed in the next hour was astounding. As I tuned in, a reporter said a contestant was about to lift 1,104 pounds. That seemed impossible to me. Even though the weightlifter was a huge human being, I could imagine that lifting that amount of weight would blow one of his knees apart, tear off an arm, or explode a vein in his head.

I have to admit, I was a bit nervous as he stepped up to the platform and stood before the bar. Suddenly he began to pound on his chest and scream. Then, as he summoned his strength, he bent down and lifted that enormous weight. Cheers of celebration followed. This athlete had accomplished what had never been done before. My son and I texted back and forth about how crazy this was.

This man had just broken a world record, but he was still limited by human weakness. He had great power, but he would never be almighty. He had trained hour after hour, day after day, month after month for year upon year. He had to train in order to defeat his weakness and build strength. He had to learn from other athletes and coaches. This huge man had to do all of this because he was a limited human being.

The most powerful things we know have limits to their power. But the reality is that when it comes to God and his power, there's no limit. And there's no comparison with any other power. To say that God is omnipotent (all-powerful) is to say that he is God.

And that means he can exercise his power, without effort, at any time and in any place he chooses. There's nothing that God cannot do, according to his holy will and pleasure. There's nothing that can stop him from exercising his power.

Behold your God!

Read: "For the LORD of hosts has purposed, and who will annul it? His hand is stretched out, and who will turn it back?" ISAIAH 14:27

Reflect: Every earthly power has limits. How does this way of thinking about power directly impact your view of God and his power?

---

2. Powerful Creator

Think with me for a moment. You have never spoken anything into existence in your entire life, and you never will. Flowers, bread, and furniture don't burst into existence at our command. What kind of power can cause things to be created with a word? And not just any kinds of things, but things with distinct beauty and perfect design?

It's stunning to read through Genesis 1 and to watch God speak the various objects and creatures of our world into existence. "Let there be light," he said, and there was light (Gen. 1:3). What? "Let the earth sprout vegetation," he said, and it was so (v. 11). Are you paying attention? "Let the waters swarm with swarms of living creatures, and let birds fly above the earth across the expanse of the heavens," he said, and it happened (v. 20). "And God saw that it was good" (v. 21). Amazing!

Human beings are creative, but we do not have the power to create. Everything we "create" begins with raw material. Even the scientists, who claim that they can generate life in a lab, always begin the process with the mixing of chemical substances. They haven't actually created anything; they have simply manipulated created substances to generate something new.

Now let your imagination loose. Look in on that moment when God took a handful of dust from the ground, breathed life into it, and created a living, breathing, thinking, relating human being, Adam. Here is one of power's highest definitions. God has the power to breathe life into something that had no life.

To say that God has the power to create and control his universe and everything in it is simply to say that he is God. There exists no one like him.

And you are his child by grace. He unleashes his power for your good. Yes, you will hit the wall of your own powerlessness, but your Lord has no such wall. There is hope for the powerless. Why? Because, in tenderness, God meets your weakness with his strength.

Read: "Now to him who is able to do far more abundantly than all that we ask or think, according to the power at work within us, to him be glory in the church and in Christ Jesus throughout all generations, forever and ever. Amen." EPHESIANS 3:20-21

Reflect: Where do you find yourself discouraged by your lack of power or ability? How can you trust God to give you what you need?

---

3. The Power of Life

When my oldest sons were three and five years old, they found a bird that was either sick or injured. They asked me if we could help it. I got a box, put tissue in it, and laid the bird in the box. While they were watching the bird, and I was thinking about what to do next, the bird died. My sons looked at me, frustrated and sad. They knew that death is final. Even at their young ages, they instinctively knew that there was nothing I could do.

We live in a world where every living thing is in the process of dying, and we can't do a single thing to stop it. So consider with me the magnificence of the resurrection of Jesus. He was in the tomb long enough to be certifiably dead. Dead.

However, rising again after death meant that the synapses in his brain suddenly began to fire; electric charges fired through his nervous system; the muscles in his heart started to pump; fresh blood coursed through his veins; his muscles suddenly became soft and flexible; his organs turned on and functioned in symmetry with one another; his eyes became moist and able to focus; he suddenly could breathe, smell, taste, and feel; and his balance and orientation returned. This is but a limited summary of everything that had to happen all at once for Jesus to be able to get up and walk alive out of that tomb.

Here's what it means to be almighty: No effort was required for Christ to rise again.

There was no consideration of whether or not it was possible. There was never a flash of doubt at any point in God's mind. He had the power to raise his Son because he is God.

This unique resurrection power of God is not just another item in our theological outline. It's at the heart of what gives us new life and future hope. Being almighty means that not even death has the power to defeat God.

Only Almighty God has the power to bring life out of what was once dead. The resurrection is a finger that points to the omnipotence of God.

Read: "I am the Alpha and the Omega," says the Lord God, "who is and who was and who is to come, the Almighty." REVELATION 1:8

Reflect: How does the resurrection of Jesus display God's almighty power?

4. Strength in Weakness

I wish I could say that I am always happy with the way God exercises his power in my life. I wish I could say that I speak only words of gratitude and never words of complaint. I wish I could say that I have never questioned the wisdom or the love behind the way God works on my behalf. Unfortunately, I go through moments of discontent. And when I do, I am tempted to look elsewhere for satisfaction.

Sadly, *we are all tempted to doubt the power of God.* At times, we all struggle to entrust our needs to the Lord, whether it's supplying our material needs, working in the hearts of our friends and family members, protecting us from temptation, or keeping us safe. You are not alone in this struggle.

Yet being a child of God means you are no longer left with the limited resources of your own power. No matter what you're facing, here is what you need to remember: God acts in power on your behalf and gifts you with power that is divine (Eph. 1:19–23).

The hope of every believer is resurrection power. The same power by which life was breathed into Christ's dead body is now yours as his child. God's power is not some distant fact. It's your hope right now. Yes, you, the one reading this right now, have been blessed with the same power that raised Christ from the dead. It is ultimate power, bigger than anything you face inside or outside of you.

You don't have the power to make people do right, but God does. You don't have the power to change hearts, but God does. You don't have the power to fix relationships, but God does. And if you believe he is with you, for you, and in you—in power—then you will live with hope. And you'll act with courage where you had been tempted to quit.

You may feel weak, but God's resolve to exercise his power—so that you have what you need—never weakens.

Read: "For the sake of Christ, then, I am content with weaknesses, insults, hardships, persecutions, and calamities. For when I am weak, then I am strong." 2 CORINTHIANS 12:10

Reflect: Where do you feel weak? How can God's power make you more confident even in your weakness?

---

5. Nothing Is Impossible

In your school, you probably have noticed that it is nearly impossible for you to love each and every one of your fellow students. For some reason, someone irritates you and causes you to feel more frustration than love. And if you have an extended family, you know that it's sometimes hard to have long-term family peace. That can be especially true at holidays.

Here's what we need to understand and be willing to confess: The Christian life is impossible.

It is impossible to love as I have been called to love.

It is impossible to forgive as I have been called to forgive.

It is impossible to serve as I have been called to serve.

It is impossible for me to guard my mind and direct my desires as I have been called to control them.

It is impossible for me to manage my tongue or harness my wandering eyes as I have been called to regulate them.

If left to myself, all of these things are impossible for me. Yet the glorious message of the gospel is that I haven't been left to myself. Read the next sentence carefully; it is a picture of how amazing God's grace really is. *God meets our weakness with his power.*

Your almighty Father's power is at work even when you are tired, discouraged, hopeless, and about to give in or give up. The rescuing, protecting, and providing power of your Savior is never idle because he never sleeps on the job. His power never stops working.

Now if you really believe this, you will quit being ruled by anxiety and worry, quit living in fear, and refuse to give up hope. If you really believe that the omnipotent power of your Lord is at work in you, then you will step into those hard places you determine to love. You will commit yourself to forgive, and you will get up and do it all again the next day.

You will do this not because you think you have power, but because your Redeemer has power beyond your ability to calculate. You will no longer be imprisoned by your weakness. Instead, you'll be freed to tap into the greatest resource of power the universe has ever known.

Read: "For nothing will be impossible with God." LUKE 1:37

Reflect: Where in your life do you need to confess weakness to God? Where has it been difficult to believe in the power of God that is at work in you?

---

6. You Are Not Enough

We all need to abandon our delusions of self-sufficiency. The lie of self-sufficiency says that you have everything you need within yourself.

Eve ate the fruit that was "desired to make one wise" (Gen. 3:6). She was after independent wisdom—a "wisdom" that didn't need to rely on God. This is why we struggle to ask for directions, to seek advice, and to submit to instruction. The theology of God's omnipotence is so helpful here.

God over and over again reveals to us that he is almighty in power precisely because we are not. We were not created to be independent. Even in a perfect world and in a perfect relationship with God, Adam and Eve were dependent on him. They did not have the power of independent wisdom or of independent strength. Sin added a whole catalog of weaknesses—weakness of heart, mind, and body—to the natural dependence of human beings. These limits were designed to drive us to the powerful God in thankful dependency and joyful submission.

Adam and Eve did not have the independent power to know how to live. They also didn't have the power to live as God commanded, apart from God's help.

Yet acknowledging your weakness will produce a greater reliance on God. And greater reliance on God will produce an enhanced awareness of his help. And a greater awareness of his help will produce a lifestyle of humble gratitude.

In contrast, when Christianity is proud and overly self-confident, it has forgotten the gospel. The good news is that God's power has come down to rescue human beings from their own weakness. Christianity that congratulates its own strength is a false gospel; it deceives those who preach it and discourages those who listen. A mature Christian is confident in weakness.

No matter what mask it wears, the gospel of self-reliance is not the gospel of the grace of the Lord Jesus Christ.

Read: "He gives power to the faint, and to him who has no might he increases strength." ISAIAH 40:29

Reflect: Where are you tempted to rely on your own strength and deny your own weakness?

---

7. Almighty Father

From the minute our children came into our family, I lived with a new sense of purpose. Parenting didn't seem burdensome to me. Suddenly there was something high on my list of values. Parenting motivated me more than most of the things in my life.

It kept me working hard. It shaped the way I invested my money, my energy, my gifts, and my time. It was in the back of my mind from the moment I awoke until I went to sleep. And many times, it was the thing that interrupted my sleep.

My children knew I loved them, but they didn't understand how much. They surely didn't know how much this one thing occupied my heart and motivated me. The moment my children entered our family, I determined to exert my fatherly power—to keep them safe and provide for their everyday needs.

One of the most encouraging ways God identifies himself is by saying this amazing thing: "I am your Father." The Lord of heaven and earth is my Father by grace. The one who sits on the throne of the universe with almighty power is my Father, and I am his child.

It seems impossible, too good to be true. Grace birthed me into God's family and, because it did, unleashed his fatherly care. Here's one of the best ways to understand the glory of God's fatherly care for his children: He exerts his power to protect us and to provide for us. *God's power is essential to his fathering care for us.*

Here is your potential: The power of your omnipotent Father is now at work within you. You are not left alone on the stage of your own little drama. You are not left to your little bag of resources.

And here's your identity: You are the son or daughter of the most powerful being in the universe. He is your Father. And he exercises his power with fatherly affection and care.

Read: "And he said, 'Abba, Father, all things are possible for you. Remove this cup from me. Yet not what I will, but what you will.'" MARK 14:36

Reflect: If you described God's power in relation to you, would you most often think of it as "fatherly"? If not, how would you describe what you most often think about his power?

6

God's Creation

What We Believe

In the beginning, it pleased God—Father, Son, and Holy Spirit—to make from nothing every visible or invisible thing that exists and to declare that all he had made was very good. He did this so his eternal power, wisdom, and goodness would be on constant display for all to see.

Why We Believe It

The passages below inform the Christian doctrine of creation. God has spoken in the Bible, so we believe what he has said there. In the following pages, we'll explore this key doctrine and what it means for us as we follow Christ.

In the beginning, God created the heavens and the earth. The earth was without form and void, and darkness was over the face of the deep. And the Spirit of God was hovering over the face of the waters.

And God said, "Let there be light," and there was light. And God saw that the light was good. And God separated the light from the darkness. God called the light Day, and the darkness he called Night. And there was evening and there was morning, the first day.

Genesis 1:1–5

You are the LORD, you alone. You have made heaven, the heaven of heavens, with all their host, the earth and all that is on it, the seas and all that is in them; and you preserve all of them; and the host of heaven worships you.

Nehemiah 9:6

O LORD, how manifold are your works!
In wisdom have you made them all;
the earth is full of your creatures.
Here is the sea, great and wide,
which teems with creatures innumerable,
living things both small and great.

Psalm 104:24–25

In the beginning was the Word, and the Word was with God, and the Word was God. He was in the beginning with God. All things were made through him, and without him was not any thing made that was made.

John 1:1–3

By him all things were created, in heaven and on earth, visible and invisible, whether thrones or dominions or rulers or authorities—all things were created through him and for him. And he is before all things, and in him all things hold together. And he is the head of the body, the church. He is the beginning, the firstborn from the dead, that in everything he might be preeminent.

Colossians 1:16–18

How It Matters

Throughout this chapter, we'll focus on the creation that God has made. In the beginning, God created the heavens and the earth, and everything they contain—all of it! He is the Creator, and we are his creatures. This changes everything and gives purpose to our lives. People were created to display God. When we understand that God is the Creator, our lives take on new meaning and our hearts overflow with grateful worship. Since he made us, he also owns us. But this doesn't make life hard for us. Instead, living under the authority of the Creator is how life was meant to be lived. And he also gives us responsibilities in his creation. Life in the Creator's world brings freedom, reminds us that we are limited, and points us to God's grace.

1. What's Your Purpose?

I have painted for decades. I have an art studio a few blocks from my house. I labor there creating artwork until it's ready for a gallery exhibition. I paint in a certain style and always with a purpose. I never begin a painting and say to myself, "I sure hope this turns into something beautiful." Why? Because before I start, I have a vision in mind. I know what I want the final product to be.

With that in mind, I lay out the steps of the process. I gather the paints, chemicals, and tools that I will need to realize my vision. Making always includes purpose.

God, the ultimate artist, designed everything he made with a purpose in mind. That includes human beings. He knew what he wanted us to be, and he knew how he wanted us to live: what he wanted us to do, how he wanted us to relate to one another and to him, and how he wanted us to interact with the rest of creation.

This means that the ultimate goal of our lives isn't happiness. The goal isn't making sure everyone loves us. The purpose of your life and mine is not material achievement, success, and affluence. The ultimate purpose is not acquiring power and control. It's not being fit and beautiful. And it's not all about loving ourselves, no matter what.

Instead, the doctrine of creation teaches us that we do not look to ourselves for purpose.

Rather, we look to our Creator. And the Creator has sent us into the world with an "owner's manual," just like the one that comes with a new car. God's manual, the Bible, lays out God's purpose for us. But it also tells us both what happens when we forsake God's purpose for our own and how he rescues and restores us through the gift of and grace of his Son.

Read: "Worthy are you, our Lord and God, to receive glory and honor and power, for you created all things, and by your will they existed and were created." REVELATION 4:11

Reflect: How do your plans and purpose for life line up with God's purpose for your life? Where do the two overlap?

---

2. Grand Opening

When you open your Bible to its beginning, the stunning, shocking, gripping account of creation is there for a reason.

Your Bible was written so that you encounter God, in all the hugeness of his glory, right away. He existed before the physical universe existed, and he spoke everything that is into existence. His glorious power, wisdom, and authority are not hidden for a moment. From the very first words of Scripture, they are spotlighted for every reader to see.

God—big, glorious, and powerfully active—dominates reality. And when faced with this incredible display of all-surpassing greatness, you can't help but feel small and weak.

This original sight-and-sound, multisensory, HD glory display was meant to astound you, to overwhelm you, and to change you. It should stimulate in you the most significant, intimate, and profound of all human functions: worship.

The Bible's account of creation is meant to drive you toward the question of why you were created. It is written to take you to the core of your humanity so you can discover your true identity. It is meant to chase into the background of your heart all the other things that would tempt you. It is designed to take you to the only place where real life will ever be found.

The words were written to make God loom so large that you drop to your knees in awe and worship. But these words were also meant to help you begin to understand your identity and place in this cosmos that this amazing one has put together.

Read: "For you formed my inward parts; you knitted me together in my mother's womb. I praise you, for I am fearfully and wonderfully made. Wonderful are your works; my soul knows it very well." PSALM 139:13-14

Reflect: As you think about your life right now, who or what is most life-giving to you? How are you allowing these delights to point you to God in worship?

---

3. Finding True Meaning in Life

You and I have to work hard to make anything. Even when you buy a piece of furniture from Ikea, with all the pieces properly designed and a booklet of instructions, it's frustrating. You're driven to the edge of your sanity trying to follow the instructions and assemble something that looks like what you thought you bought.

All of our do-it-yourself projects require mental focus, physical skill, and perseverance. We struggle to make things, even though we always start with raw materials, follow instructions, and have the appropriate tools. But you and I have never *created* anything; we do not make something out of nothing.

In contrast, God, with nothing more than his will and his word—literally, no exaggeration here—spoke the universe into existence. Think of huge galaxies and little ants. Think of flowing bodies of water and hardened shafts of granite. Think of the body of an elephant and the translucent creatures that swim in the deepest trenches of the sea. Think of huge, towering trees and microscopic organisms. Think of the technology of the human eye and the intricate design of your hand. Think of sound waves and chemical reactions.

Genesis 1 and 2 are meant to put you in your place and insert God in his proper place in your heart and life. The words of Genesis 1:1—"In the beginning, God created the heavens and the earth"—define and explain everything. They give you identity and dignity. They define the meaning and purpose of life.

The truth of creation should stop us in our tracks. It should fill us with awe and wonder, humble us, and drop us to our knees.

Read: "By faith we understand that the universe was created by the word of God, so that what is seen was not made out of things that are visible." HEBREWS 11:3

Reflect: Which detail about God's creation (listed above) stood out to you most? Why? Give thanks to God for his astounding creation.

---

4. Responding in Worship

God created the world, so everything is defined by that reality. It also means that the Creator is worthy of our constant awe, submission, and obedience.

But most of us have a problem. I am afraid the doctrine of creation has become so familiar to us that it no longer moves us in the way it should. Sometimes, when we bump across something with which we are familiar, our minds tend to quit thinking, our eyes tend to quit looking, and our hearts tend to stop responding. It's sad when considering something like the doctrine of creation becomes just a mental exercise. How tragic when creation no longer fills our minds with wonder and our hearts with worship.

Instead, every glorious created thing was designed by God to be a finger that points to his glory. We need to pray for grace that we would always see the glorious one who is behind the glorious physical thing we are seeing, hearing, tasting, or touching.

How can we boil water, mash potatoes, or scramble eggs without seeing the glory of God?

How can we hold an infant in our arms without being in awe of her Creator?

How can the ever-changing variety of hues of a sunset not produce awe of God in us?

How can tadpoles in a stream not make us smile in worship?

How can the whistle of wind through the trees not become a hymn of praise in our hearts to God?

Look around at the glory display that is available to us every day. If we don't see God, we are profoundly needy human beings. We desperately need the eye-opening, heart-enlivening rescue of God's grace. Call on his grace to open your eyes and your heart to the glory that's everywhere around you.

Read: "There is one God, the Father, from whom are all things and for whom we exist, and one Lord, Jesus Christ, through whom are all things and through whom we exist." 1 CORINTHIANS 8:6

Reflect: When was the last time you stopped to marvel at God's amazing creation? How can marveling at his creation lead you to worship?

---

5. You Are Not Your Own

When I finish a painting, it belongs to me. Nobody questions that. I own every painting in my studio or hanging in an exhibit—until it's purchased by someone else.

This is the logic of creation: You make it, you own it.

So it is with God's creation of the world and everything in it. The physical universe belongs to the Lord. It was created by him and for him (Rom. 11:36). God is the rightful owner of all things.

So treating the physical world as if it belongs to you—to do with whatever you want—never goes anywhere good. Trees, flowers, streams, the sky, the air, the wind and the rains, the sand and the sea, mountains and valleys, birds, cows in the field, and the dog under your table all belong to the Lord. It's humbling to understand that you are not the owner; you are simply the resident manager.

This means we must steward the plants, animals, land, air, and water with a humble recognition that they don't belong to us. As humble and thankful resident managers, we should give ourselves to care for what belongs to someone else. Why? So that he will be pleased and get the credit that is due to him alone.

This stewardship doesn't extend just to our physical environment but to each other as well. We are called to represent God's love and care for all those made in his image. Because we're his resident managers, we must take seriously our calling to one another. We should show God's love, justice, compassion, mercy, protection, and provision.

God's Creator ownership calls us to one more thing. It's important to remind yourself, every morning of your life, that *you* don't belong to you either. I don't own my rationality, spirituality, personality, emotionality, physicality, psychology, gifts, or volition. I am to steward all of life for God and for his purpose.

A life well lived is a life based on the understanding that you don't belong to you.

Read: "Do you not know that your body is a temple of the Holy Spirit within you, whom you have from God? You are not your own, for you were bought with a price. So glorify God in your body." 1 CORINTHIANS 6:19–20

Reflect: When people look at your life, how are they able to practically see that you belong to God?

6. Take Me to Your Leader

A long time ago, my mom and dad moved to Southern California and became the resident managers of a large apartment complex. They owned nothing there, not even the apartment where they lived. But they had been tasked with both caring for the property and also overseeing how the renters took care of the property. My mom and dad couldn't treat the place like it belonged to them. They couldn't do whatever they wanted with the grounds or the renters. They were employed to steward the complex according to the plans, purposes, and rules of the owners.

Still, my mom and dad had authority, and the renters knew it. They exercised their authority in various ways every day. Sometimes their authority was welcomed. Other times it was resisted. Yet they were faithful to use their authority as needed.

The thing they didn't have was ultimate authority. My parents did not have the right to exercise their authority however they wished. Why? Because they didn't own the complex.

This is where the doctrine of creation leads us when it comes to authority. Since God made the world and owns it, he is the ultimate authority over everything.

This means that you do not have the right to use your power and position however you want. Every expression of human authority should represent God's values, purposes, and character (Rom. 13:1).

Wouldn't homes be safer and more loving places if parents were like this? Wouldn't the classroom work better if teachers understood this? Wouldn't government function better for the good of its citizens if every elected official saw himself or herself as a representative of God?

God is the ultimate authority. All other authority looks to him for its character and purpose. It is vital to remember that there is no such thing as human authority that is not answerable to God. So we can rest. Why? Not because the human authorities over us are always good, loving, and wise. Rather, we can rest because our Creator Lord is the final authority. And he is holy in every way and boundless in love.

Read: "Oh come, let us worship and bow down; let us kneel before the LORD, our Maker!" PSALM 95:6

Reflect: What has God the Creator given to you for you to steward? Under God's authority, what do you feel responsible to manage and care for in life?

7. True Freedom

The doctrine of creation is meant to release us from our bondage to us. It is meant to welcome us out of the prison of our own self-centeredness.

Genesis 1 and 2 remind us that the great narrative of the cosmos didn't begin with us. The most amazing thing that ever happened, happened without us.

The doctrine of creation reminds me that I am not at the center of what is. God is not only the great author of the story of life. He is also the principal actor, the great star who dominates the stage and compels our attention. Everything comes from him, everything points to him, and everything continues to him. He gets the spotlight and takes home the honors. There is no greatness debate to be had. There is no one who could seriously claim to be his equal. All creation bows to his majesty.

Here's where the humbling process of grace begins. As you begin to bow to God's centrality and confess your smallness and dependency, you begin to be free from the dangerous delusions of your own majesty.

Here's where you begin to forsake your reliance on your own wisdom and power. Here's where you quit trying to write your own story. Here's where you start to be free from being obsessed with your own glory. Here's where you begin to escape your constant need to be right, to be in control, and to be acclaimed. Here's where you give up writing your own rules. Here's where you let go of thinking that you're smart enough to plan your own life.

Divine love confronts you with God: big, dominant, and all-surpassing. In humbling you, God extends to you his grace. What is written in the creation accounts is not just for his glory; it is also for your eternal good. Creation is on display because redeeming grace is God's plan.

Read: "His invisible attributes, namely, his eternal power and divine nature, have been clearly perceived, ever since the creation of the world, in the things that have been made." ROMANS 1:20

Reflect: When you stand before a beautiful lake or majestic mountain, why do thoughts about yourself tend to disappear into the background?

7

God's Image

What We Believe

After God had made all other creatures, he created people—male and female. He created them with eternal souls and designed them after his own image. Adam and Eve were created with the power to fulfill God's law, which was written on their hearts. Yet they also had the possibility of disobeying. Besides the law that was written in their hearts, God commanded them not to eat of the tree of the knowledge of good and evil. During the time they obeyed this command, they were happy in their communion with God.

Why We Believe It

The passages below inform the Christian doctrine of man's creation in the image of God. God has spoken in the Bible, so we believe what he has said there. In the following pages, we'll explore this key doctrine and what it means for us as we follow Christ.

Then God said, "Let us make man in our image, after our likeness. And let them have dominion over the fish of the sea and over the birds of the heavens and over the livestock and over all the earth and over every creeping thing that creeps on the earth."

So God created man in his own image,
in the image of God he created him;
male and female he created them.

And God blessed them. And God said to them, "Be fruitful and multiply and fill the earth and subdue it, and have dominion over the fish of the sea and over the birds of the heavens and over every living thing that moves on the earth."

Genesis 1:26–28

And he made from one man every nation of mankind to live on all the face of the earth, having determined allotted periods and the boundaries of their dwelling place, that they should seek God, and perhaps feel their way toward him and find him. Yet he is actually not far from each one of us, for

> "In him we live and move and have our being";
> as even some of your own poets have said,
> "For we are indeed his offspring."

Acts 17:26–28

Be renewed in the spirit of your minds, and . . . put on the new self, created after the likeness of God in true righteousness and holiness.

Therefore, having put away falsehood, let each one of you speak the truth with his neighbor, for we are members one of another. Be angry and do not sin; do not let the sun go down on your anger, and give no opportunity to the devil. Let the thief no longer steal, but rather let him labor, doing honest work with his own hands, so that he may have something to share with anyone in need. Let no corrupting talk come out of your mouths, but only such as is good for building up, as fits the occasion, that it may give grace to those who hear. And do not grieve the Holy Spirit of God, by whom you were sealed for the day of redemption. Let all bitterness and wrath and anger and clamor and slander be put away from you, along with all malice. Be kind to one another, tenderhearted, forgiving one another, as God in Christ forgave you.

Ephesians 4:23–32

No human being can tame the tongue. It is a restless evil, full of deadly poison. With it we bless our Lord and Father, and with it we curse people who are made in the likeness of God. From the same mouth come blessing and cursing. My brothers, these things ought not to be so.

James 3:8–10

How It Matters

Throughout this chapter, we'll focus on how God created humans in his image. Being made in the image of God gives humans a value, dignity, and worth that far exceeds any other part of creation. No one earns this worth—it's given to all humans by God. And this value doesn't change from person to person because we're all equally made in the image of our Creator. He made us in his likeness for amazing purposes. Since he is himself triune, one God in three persons, he created us in his image so that we might enjoy relationships and community. He made us for himself—to worship and enjoy him. He made us to rule over his good world—in wisdom and love. And when we fail to live up to God's purpose for us, we see Jesus—who is the perfect image of God. In him we have both our example and our only hope for grace.

1. Unearned Worth and Dignity

Luella and I had been waiting for the day when we would receive the little girl we were adopting. She had been assigned to us at birth, but we had to wait four long months to finally hold her in our arms.

I will never forget the sight of our caseworker walking from the airplane. She was carrying our new little one, face forward. We could see her and she could see us. The caseworker walked over to me, placed this tiny little human being in my arms, and then stepped away.

It was a thunderous moment. I had been handed a real, living human being. She had been placed in my hands for me to love, nurture, instruct, guide, provide for, and protect. I told her how much I loved her as tears streamed down my face. I stood in that holy moment holding this little, dependent, and defenseless baby girl. She was brimming with dignity, significance, and value. Why? Because stamped on her was the image of God himself. My hands trembled as my heart worked to take it all in.

We had a lot of pets in our house, from geckos to Jack Russell terriers. It was always a bit amazing when we would bring a new animal home. It was fun to bond with new pets and watch them develop. Yet those experiences were nothing like that incredible moment in the airport.

So when God describes people in Genesis 1, his reference to his "likeness" is amazing. And "in his own image" is a profound announcement. With those words, God is defining the identity of humans. He's communicating the uniqueness of their relationship to him.

Adam and Eve are not just part of the catalog of creatures that God made. They are above, they are special, and they are blessed with a dignity that separates them from everything else. By saying they are made in his likeness, God names the unchanging worth of people. This worth is never earned and cannot be taken away.

Our society often attaches a woman's worth to her beauty. When it comes to the value, dignity, significance, and uniqueness of the imprint of the image of God, men and women are equals (read Gen. 1:27 below). To reduce a woman down to the shape of her body, to negate the value of her God-given contribution as one of his image bearers, dishonors not only her but God himself. We want boys to grow into men who value the presence and gifts of women in the body of Christ. And we want girls to be clear about their calling and the need to hone the gifts God has given them.

To be human is to have dignity and worth because you carry the image of God himself.

Read: "So God created man in his own image, in the image of God he created him; male and female he created them." GENESIS 1:27

Reflect: Are there certain people you value (or devalue) because of what they're like or how they appear?

2. Does Every Human Have the Same Worth?

Human value is not achieved by success. It is not the product of your race. Human value is not the result of your money, power, or control. It's not a matter of how fit and attractive you are. Human value is not about intellectual, athletic, or artistic ability. It is not a matter of your personality or your talents.

When we think that human worth is attained by one of these factors, bad things happen. We end up doing things to one another when we forget that every human being has the same value because every human being is made in the image of God.

The most powerful leader in the world and the lowliest person in the world are both made in God's image. Men and women and boys and girls equally share his image. The hyperfit athlete and the frail elderly woman are alike in that they are made in God's image. The rebellious teenager and the self-conscious middle schooler are both image bearers.

Racists and civil-rights activists share this same foundational identity. The doctor and the patient, the worker and the boss, the homeless man and the rich man, the pastor and his people, the government official and the ordinary citizen, the person who lives in Paris and the child born in the Andes—all of them have God's image forever stamped on them.

Look into the face of any person and remember the one thing you know for sure about him or her: That person bears the stamp of God's image. Everything you think about people and all the ways that you would relate to them should be shaped by God's declaration that people are made "*in his own image.*"

Read: "Then the LORD God formed the man of dust from the ground and breathed into his nostrils the breath of life, and the man became a living creature." GENESIS 2:7

Reflect: Why do you think some people minimize the truth that every human is made in God's image?

GOD'S IMAGE   85

3. We Were Made for Community

Unlike my wife, I'm naturally shy. So when Luella and I attend a party, in ten minutes Luella is best friends with everyone, and I'm off in a corner hoping no one talks to me.

But God did not design me to live an independent, isolated life. Relationships are an essential part of the way the Creator perfectly designed people. We see it in the very beginning, when God declared that he had made Adam and Eve in his image and likeness.

God is the ultimate relational being. No, I don't mean that God needs relationships with us. He is self-sufficient, needing nothing outside of himself. What I mean is that God *is* a community. Father, Son, and Holy Spirit dwell in a relationship of perfect communion with one another.

So to be made in the image of God surely means that we are made for community. I will fully live out of the image that the Creator has stamped on me only when I love God above all else and love my neighbor as myself.

Let's be honest here: Sin makes this unnatural for all of us. We *are* relational, but we make life all about us. Rather than worshiping God, we insert ourselves into God's position. And rather than loving people, we use them to get the things that we love. We all do this in some way.

So the relational nature of the image of God shows us our need for the gospel of the grace of Jesus. At the heart of believing that you were made in the image of God is living a life of both vertical and horizontal love (1 Cor. 13).

We were designed to be like God; that is, to live in communities of unity and love. May we humbly confess our selfishness and seek the grace we need to live in this way.

Read: "Anyone who does not love does not know God, because God is love." 1 JOHN 4:8

Reflect: Prayerfully consider whom God might want you to show love to this week and how you can do it.

4. We Were Made to Be Holy

Imagine you are shopping in a busy mall. In front of you is an elderly lady, leaning on a cane and walking with difficulty. Then, all of a sudden, a kid tears through the crowd, knocking the elderly lady down, taking her purse, and running away. Some people in the crowd run after the kid while others seek to give the lady aid and comfort, but everyone is thinking the same thing: "What that kid did to that lady was wrong."

What's going on at that moment? It's God-designed moral awareness. No, it's not perfect, but it is still there. Everyone thinks about right and wrong, and carries around with them some kind of moral code.

In the Bible, we read that until Adam and Eve rebelled against God's wise and loving command, they were perfect in righteousness and holiness (Eccl. 7:29). Human beings were created by God as moral beings. They had the law of God written on their hearts. This means they were born with a sense of some standards of right and wrong. Human perfection was shattered in that moment of rebellion in the garden, but our moral hardwiring still exists.

Yet the rules by which most people live have been divorced from the perfectly holy wisdom of the Creator. Yes, there are moments, such as that one in the mall, when moral awareness operates well. But we won't do well if we repudiate God's law, remove the concept of sin from our vocabulary, and write laws of our own making.

Once again, this points us to the cross of Jesus. He perfectly obeyed the law on our behalf and took on the penalty for our sin. On the cross, he purchased a new heart and a renewed mind for us. His grace empowers us to obey and his work guarantees that we will one day be like him. Then we will live with him in perfect righteousness and holiness forever and ever. What is now broken in us will, by grace, be fully restored.

Read: "For when Gentiles, who do not have the law, by nature do what the law requires, they are a law to themselves, even though they do not have the law. They show that the work of the law is written on their hearts." ROMANS 2:14–15

Reflect: When unbelievers tell you that Christianity is wrong, you can ask them how they know that. When they share their opinion about right and wrong, aren't they actually telling you what *they believe*?

5. We Were Made for God

That morning at the airport, when our daughter, at just four months of age, was placed in our arms, we were thunderstruck. We were overwhelmed with wonder, with the depth of our responsibility, and with all the emotions that resulted.

What really blew us away was that God had called us to care for the soul of this little one. Because she was made in the image of God, she was, in her essence, a spiritual being like him.

God designed this little one to be able to know him, relate to him, love him, talk to him, and worship him. These capacities separated Adam and Eve from the rest of creation—and the same is true for every human being. Our little girl was made for God. She was made to live with him; she was made to listen to him. She was made to obey God, and she was made to offer her heart to him in awe, wonder, and worship.

Yet because we are spiritual beings, we often name things as "god" that are not God. Because we are worshipers, we will always hook our hopes and dreams to something. Wired with imaginations, we envision what life will be like if this "god" will come through for us. Children do it; husbands and wives do it; students, friends, and grandparents do it. Everyone is on a great life-shaping spiritual search. Yet the misuse of these spiritual capacities is itself an argument for how much we need Jesus Christ.

We were designed to communicate so we could talk to God. We were given mental abilities so we could think about what God has said to us and apply it to our daily lives. We were given emotions so we would be able to experience the joy of loving God and being loved by him, and so we could hate what God hates. We were built with the capacity to worship so our hearts would be drawn to the Lord in gratitude, wonder, and praise.

All of these abilities are ours because we, made in the image of God, are spiritual beings. And we were made to be able to live Godward lives.

Read: "Set your minds on things that are above, not on things that are on earth. For you have died, and your life is hidden with Christ in God. When Christ who is your life appears, then you also will appear with him in glory." COLOSSIANS 3:2-4

Reflect: Where are you most often tempted to allow your heart to be drawn to worship something other than God?

6. We Were Meant to Rule

We are not just part of creation. We have been designed for a unique leadership role.

Read carefully the flow of the language in Genesis 1:26: "Then God said, 'Let us make man in our image, after our likeness. And let them have dominion.'" The most immediate and clear definition of what it means to be made in the image of God is to "have dominion."

To be made in God's image is to be made for ruling.

Yet human beings were not made for independent rule. By ruling, they're obeying the Creator. God says, "This is how I have designed you. This is what I have created you for, and this is what I want you to do." We're agents of God's rule on earth.

So when we rule, we display the existence and values of the one who created and commissioned us. In every area of human life, we are meant to rule in a way that represents God. His design is to make his invisible rule visible.

I have a confession to make. I don't get up every morning and ask myself how I might make his rule visible. I don't ask how I might represent the heart, story, and plan of God in the situations, locations, and relationships that occupy me throughout the day.

I am, however, filled with the urgency of many things that are important to me. That can include tasks that I want to complete, plans that I would like to accomplish, or pleasures that I would love to enjoy.

It's easy to forget that God has stamped "Agent" on me. Yet this is who I am and it is how I am meant to live. And because it is, I am in constant need of his rescuing and empowering grace. I suspect you are too.

Read: "You have made [man] a little lower than the heavenly beings and crowned him with glory and honor. You have given him dominion over the works of your hands; you have put all things under his feet." PSALM 8:5-6

Reflect: What areas of your life reflect God's rule the most? What areas might not reflect it so well?

7. Jesus, the Perfect Image of God

No aspect of our image-bearing functions as God intended. It all has been bent and twisted by sin. You can see the stamp of the glory of God on us. Yet its reflection has been dimmed by the dirt and damage of sin.

In contrast, the image of God is most powerfully seen in the Son of God, the Son of Man, Jesus Christ. In the flesh, Jesus stands before us as the ultimate image bearer. In him, the image is not dented or damaged in any way. In him, we see God's image in perfect expression in every decision, every word, every thought, every desire, and every aspect of his character, all spotlessly righteous.

In him, we can observe the image of God in its ultimate expression: the Messiah man, Jesus. And that should fill us with enthusiasm and hope. He is a living representation of what we will one day be, when the burden of sin has been fully lifted. On that day, the image of God will be given full expression in us in every way and all of the time.

When you see the perfect expression of the image of God in Jesus, it should also break your heart. We should weep at the damage sin has done. You're confronted with it in yourself and all around you every day. When it comes to the image of God imprinted on us, things are not the way they were meant to be.

Similarly, Scripture doesn't call us to "just preach the gospel." No, it calls us to tirelessly preach the gospel while we tirelessly work as God's agents of mercy and justice (Matt. 23:23). We cannot stand silent while any image bearer is denigrated, oppressed, devalued, or living with regular injustices. Because every human being is an image bearer, every act of injustice is sin against the honor and authority of God.

Through the life, death, and resurrection of Jesus, the ultimate image bearer, God begins the process of restoring his image in all who believe. The work of Jesus on our behalf is a promise of more. It's a guarantee that one day God's image in us will be fully restored. A day is coming when, by the grace of Jesus, we will be more fully human than we have ever been.

Read: "And we all, with unveiled face, beholding the glory of the Lord, are being transformed into the same image from one degree of glory to another. For this comes from the Lord who is the Spirit." 2 CORINTHIANS 3:18

Reflect: Where does the brokenness of this good world break your heart the most? Why? And how is Jesus the ultimate answer to that brokenness?

8

Sin

What We Believe

The first humans, Adam and Eve, were deceived by Satan to eat the forbidden fruit, leading to the loss of their original righteousness, communion with God, and life itself. As a result, all of humanity inherits sin, guilt, and corruption. We became wholly inclined to evil and resistant to good. This original corruption is the source of all sin and continues even in Christians. Each sin breaks God's law and makes the sinner guilty and subject to God's wrath and the law's curse. These bring spiritual, temporal, and eternal suffering.

Why We Believe It

The passages below inform the Christian doctrine of sin. God has spoken in the Bible, so we believe what he has said there. In the following pages, we'll explore this key doctrine and what it means for us as we follow Christ.

And the LORD God commanded the man, saying, "You may surely eat of every tree of the garden, but of the tree of the knowledge of good and evil you shall not eat, for in the day that you eat of it you shall surely die."

Genesis 2:16–17

Have mercy on me, O God,
    according to your steadfast love;
according to your abundant mercy
    blot out my transgressions.
Wash me thoroughly from my iniquity,
    and cleanse me from my sin!
For I know my transgressions,
    and my sin is ever before me.
Against you, you only, have I sinned
    and done what is evil in your sight,
so that you may be justified in your words
    and blameless in your judgment.
Behold, I was brought forth in iniquity,
    and in sin did my mother conceive me.

Psalm 51:1–5

For no good tree bears bad fruit, nor again does a bad tree bear good fruit, for each tree is known by its own fruit. For figs are not gathered from thornbushes, nor are grapes picked from a bramble bush. The good person out of the good treasure of his heart produces good, and the evil person out of his evil treasure produces evil, for out of the abundance of the heart his mouth speaks.

Luke 6:43–45

Therefore, just as sin came into the world through one man, and death through sin, and so death spread to all men because all sinned—for sin indeed was in the world before the law was given, but sin is not counted where there is no law. Yet death reigned from Adam to Moses, even over those whose sinning was not like the transgression of Adam, who was a type of the one who was to come.

But the free gift is not like the trespass. For if many died through one man's trespass, much more have the grace of God and the free gift by the grace of that one man Jesus Christ abounded for many. And the free gift is not like the result of that one man's sin. For the judgment following one trespass brought condemnation, but the free gift following many trespasses brought justification. For if, because of one man's trespass, death reigned through that one man, much more will those who receive the abundance of grace and the free gift of righteousness reign in life through the one man Jesus Christ.

Romans 5:12–17

How It Matters

 Throughout this chapter, we'll focus on the Bible's teaching about sin. This is the greatest problem in the world—the cancer that's at the heart of every problem. It all started for humans when Adam and Eve sinned. Ever since their disobedience against God, every human being is born a sinner. We were made to worship God, but instead—because of sin—we worship ourselves. Yet on our own, we don't see the real problem. Sin blinds us to our own sinfulness. And it gets worse—sin also enslaves us and hurts our relationships. Yet there's hope in Jesus Christ. He forgives us, rescues us from sin's penalty and power, and transforms our hearts.

1. What's the Problem?

Sin is everywhere you look. You don't have to do a deep-dive analysis to see its trouble in you and all around you. It twists and distorts every good thing that God created. We see sin and brokenness in gender confusion, human trafficking, marriages lurching toward divorce, domestic violence, terrorism and war, political corruption, the unborn being ripped from the womb, poverty, racial injustice, violence in the streets, and a host of other global problems.

We will never solve these problems without a deeply biblical and comprehensively applied theology of sin.

The Bible's teaching about sin lies at the very center of Christian doctrine. It's a significant worldview watershed. If you believe there is no such thing as sin, you will see no need for God's moral law or the wisdom of Scripture. You won't see your need to depend on God or on the rescuing grace of the Redeemer.

One of the sad results of sin is that the average sinner on the street carries with him little, if any, awareness of sin, understanding of it, or feelings of guilt because of it. Sin is no longer a category in most people's minds or in American culture. The truth of human sinfulness doesn't shape the way most people think.

If you do not believe that sin affects everything (and in terrible ways), then you think that humans have the power to fix humans. So you put your hope in education, politics, philosophy, psychology, medicine, and so on. All of these things are beneficial. Yet they can't rescue us from the darkness, deceit, destruction, and death that sin has rained down on us all.

If, however, you believe that the deepest problem for every human being is sin, then you know that together we cannot save ourselves. If there is such a thing as sin inside the heart of everyone, then our only hope is God and his redeeming, rescuing, and restoring grace.

If sin is the ultimate cancer, then there is no cure to be found outside of the grace of the Redeemer.

Read: "But God, being rich in mercy, because of the great love with which he loved us, even when we were dead in our trespasses, made us alive together with Christ—by grace you have been saved." EPHESIANS 2:4–5

Reflect: Where do you think most people place the blame for the problems in today's world? How would you answer them?

2. How Did We Get into This Mess?

The first people God made—Adam and Eve—were seduced by the lies of Satan. They sinned in eating the fruit that God had forbidden. Because of this sin, they fell from their original righteousness and communion with God. The results were awful. Adam and Eve became dead in sin and completely corrupt in every faculty and every part of their souls and bodies.

But what about us today? This will take your breath away. Did you know that Adam and Eve's selfish, idolatrous, and rebellious choice in the garden cursed every human being who has followed them? Yes, that includes even you and me.

The disaster is not only that Adam and Eve were punished for their sin; it is also that, because of sin, they became completely different people. No longer perfectly righteous in word, thought, and action, they were corrupt in every way. No longer lovers of God and his law, Adam and Eve were separated from God and attracted to what is evil in his sight. And all of this was passed down to their children and their children's children and every generation that followed.

This means that sin is the ultimate bomb, leaving a trail of destruction in its path. Sin is the ultimate pandemic, infecting everyone, leaving everyone sick. Sin is the ultimate curse, sentencing everyone to death. Sin is the ultimate deceit, telling you endless lies and making promises it can't keep. Sin is the ultimate interruption, changing the human story forever.

And if sin is the problem—our problem—then God is our only hope.

Read: "Therefore, as one trespass led to condemnation for all men, so one act of righteousness leads to justification and life for all men. For as by the one man's disobedience the many were made sinners, so by the one man's obedience the many will be made righteous." ROMANS 5:18-19

Reflect: Which analogy given above ("ultimate bomb," "ultimate curse," etc.) was most meaningful to you? Why?

---

3. Everyone Worships

When it comes to sin, hopelessness is the only doorway to hope. Do you want to enjoy the delivering grace of God through his Son, Jesus? Then you need to abandon any hope of defeating sin by your own ability.

Here's why: I can run from situations, locations, and relationships, but I cannot run from myself. And from the beginning, the human problem has been the human heart.

In the garden, for the very first time, Eve worshiped something other than God. The thing that replaced God in the worship of Eve's heart was Eve. Love of self replaced love for God. As a result, Eve rebelled against the clear, wise, and loving command of God. She ate what was forbidden. So sin at its heart worships self. And this is the idol from which every other form of idolatry flows.

If you worship yourself, you will then exchange worship and service of God for worship and service of created things.

If you worship yourself, you will then bow before the idols of comfort and pleasure.

SIN 97

If you worship yourself, your heart will be ruled by a desire for power and control.

If you worship yourself, you will crave the praise of people.

At the base of all forms of human dysfunction is the idol of self. Every sin is idolatrous; it puts us on God's throne, sovereign over our own lives and doing what we want. So it was right for David to confess to God, "Against you, you only, have I sinned and done what is evil in your sight" (Ps. 51:4).

And that means the only hope for me is a powerful Savior, who has the willingness and the might to free me from my bondage to me. Sin is not just a matter of behavior, but is also a matter of worship. That means hope for sinners is only ever found in the person and work of the Redeemer, Jesus Christ.

Read: "Wretched man that I am! Who will deliver me from this body of death? Thanks be to God through Jesus Christ our Lord! So then, I myself serve the law of God with my mind, but with my flesh I serve the law of sin. There is therefore now no condemnation for those who are in Christ Jesus." ROMANS 7:24–8:1

Reflect: Why do we as humans believe that God himself, his wisdom, and his goodness won't be enough for us?

---

4. Are You Blind?

One of the most devastatingly dangerous powers of sin is its ability to deceive. Sin is an evil monster masquerading as your best friend. It is a grim reaper masquerading as a life giver. Sin is darkness masquerading as light. It is foolishness masquerading as wisdom. Sin is disease masquerading as a cure. It is a trap masquerading as a gift.

No matter how it presents itself to you, sin is never what it appears to be and will never deliver what it promises.

Sin is deceptive because it presents as beautiful what God says is ugly. When you are on your third burger, you are not seeing the danger of gluttony. Instead, you are experiencing the pleasure of succulent meat, dripping cheese, and that soft bun. When materialism has you spending money that you don't have on things you don't need, you are not feeling the danger of your greed and thievery. Instead, you are taken up with the pleasure of your new things.

Sin is also deceptive because it lulls us into minimizing our transgressions. We fall into thinking that our anger doesn't matter, that the little lie doesn't make much of a difference, that our gossip won't hurt anyone, that our impatience isn't a big deal, or that everyone is envious once in a while. Because of sin, we try to convince ourselves that our sin isn't that sinful after all.

But notice the remedy for spiritual blindness that's given in the passage from Hebrews (below): "Exhort one another every day." This is very humbling. We're so easily tricked that we require daily intervention.

To help with our spiritual blindness, we need instruments of seeing in our lives. We need others' eyes to help us see what we cannot.

And in his grace, God has surrounded you in his church with instruments of seeing. So open your heart to his gracious provision, and you'll have a defense against the blinding power of sin.

Read: "Take care, brothers, lest there be in any of you an evil, unbelieving heart, leading you to fall away from the living God. But exhort one another every day, as long as it is called 'today,' that none of you may be hardened by the deceitfulness of sin." HEBREWS 3:12–13

Reflect: Who are two people that are speaking truth into your life? Are you listening to their warnings or ignoring them? Why?

5. Slaves of Sin

Sin is not just attractive, presenting as beautiful what God says is ugly, but it is also addictive. Sin is more than a bad thing you do; it is a master. And if you welcome it into your life, it has the dark power to enslave you. Somehow, someway, sin turns us all into addicts.

Hear the words of Jesus: "Truly, truly, I say to you, everyone who practices sin is a slave to sin" (John 8:34). The pleasures of sin pass quickly, but its mastery over you remains. Because sin gives you momentary pleasure, you reach out for what God forbids. But the pleasure quickly fades. So you reach out again, hungry for more because created things have no ability to satisfy your heart.

Each time you reach out for more, you need more to achieve the pleasure you are craving. Whether it's gluttony, materialism, gossip, stealing, the desire for power and control, or the craving for appreciation and success, what temporarily satisfied you yesterday doesn't do so today. You have to have more and more.

Before long you can't stop thinking about the object of your sinful craving. What you once were convinced was harmless and under your control now controls you. You are addicted to what God has forbidden.

Sin is never harmless; it is a cruel slave master, out to kidnap your heart and control your life.

The addicting and enslaving power of sin should make each of us thankful for the power of the Messiah. Jesus is powerful to "proclaim liberty to the captives, and the opening of the prison to those who are bound" (Isa. 61:1). He is our only hope of escape from the bondage-inducing power of sin.

Do you need to run to your Savior for his bondage-breaking grace? He is able, he is willing, and he will not turn you away.

Read: "Do you not know that if you present yourselves to anyone as obedient slaves, you are slaves of the one whom you obey, either of sin, which leads to death, or of obedience, which leads to righteousness?" ROMANS 6:16

Reflect: Where do you feel drawn to sin, craving its pleasure (and never being truly satisfied)? Confess this sin and addiction to Jesus, the only Master who can free you.

---

6. Sin Hurts Our Relationships

Why do we get so impatient with or so irritated by the people we say we love? Why do human relationships become dark, violent, and abusive? Why do we have such a hard time getting along?

No passage more directly addresses these questions than James 4:1–4 (below).

Stop now and read the passage below, then think about what James is telling us. Our relationships are made difficult because of our sinful passions (desires). For example, I want something, but you are in the way of it, so I am instantly angry with you. Sin sets relationships on fire. Ask yourself:

Why do we get angry in traffic?

Why do we get upset when someone disagrees with us?

Why does it make us mad when someone makes us wait?

Why do our parents and siblings irritate us?

Why does conflict mess up our holidays and family gatherings?

Why do children fight on the playground?

Why do husbands and wives quarrel?

Why do neighbors find it hard to live at peace with one another?

All of these questions are answered by the brilliance of James's analysis of sin. James is helping us to understand that we bring our heart problems into our interactions with other people. Each one of us drags the selfishness of sin into every one of our relationships.

Here's James's argument: If we're ever going to experience peace in our relationships, we first need to have our heart problems fixed. Vertical confession (to God) has the power to produce horizontal peace (with other people), and for that we need help.

Because sin makes such a huge mess of our relationships, our only solution is the rescuing intervention of God's grace.

Read: "What causes quarrels and what causes fights among you? Is it not this, that your passions are at war within you? You desire and do not have, so you murder. You covet and cannot obtain, so you fight and quarrel. You do not have, because you do not ask. You ask and do not receive, because you ask wrongly, to spend it on your passions. You adulterous people! Do you not know that friendship with the world is enmity with God?" JAMES 4:1–4

Reflect: What would your story be like, what would your life be like, and what would your relationships be like if they were not stained and twisted by sin?

7. Hope for the Sinful Heart

If our problem were simply that we do wrong things, then changing our actions would fix it. But what if sin is, in fact, a problem of the heart? Then lasting change in a person's behavior will always travel through the pathway of the heart.

Rules can't change us. The gospel tells us that if God's law had the power to rescue and transform our hearts, Jesus would not have had to come. And people can't change us. No human being has the power to transform another person. A truly changed heart is always the result of God's grace.

God says, "And I will give you a new heart, and a new spirit I will put within you. And I will remove the heart of stone from your flesh and give you a heart of flesh" (Ezek. 36:26).

SIN 101

The word picture here is very helpful. If I have a stone in my hands and I squeeze it with all my might, nothing happens. Why? Because it's hard and resistant to change. But a soft, fleshy object is malleable; it can be molded into any shape I desire. The promise of the gospel is heart change, without which there is no victory over sin.

We like to make plans for self-reformation. We think:

"I will do better next time."

"It was just a weak moment."

"I'm smarter now than I was."

"I think I know what to do next time."

"I now know how to avoid this in the future."

But the fact that sin always originates in the heart destroys those plans. Instead, we must humbly confess that when it comes to sin, our biggest problem is us. We are led astray not primarily by things outside of us but by the thoughts, desires, motivations, cravings, and choices of our own hearts. We also have no power whatsoever to change our hearts or the heart of anyone else.

Lasting change is only ever an act of divine grace. So we run to our Savior for the rescue and transformation that only he can provide.

Read: "Since therefore the children share in flesh and blood, he himself likewise partook of the same things, that through death he might destroy the one who has the power of death, that is, the devil, and deliver all those who through fear of death were subject to lifelong slavery." HEBREWS 2:14–15

Reflect: Think about this: Why can't you change your heart? Why can only Jesus change your desires and transform you on the inside?

9

Justification

What We Believe

Those whom God calls, he justifies—by declaring that Christ's obedience and sacrifice for our sin count as ours. So by faith, we need to receive, accept, and rest in Christ as the sole means of our justification. It is a gift of God to us. And God continues to forgive the sins of all who are justified. The faith that justifies is not a dead faith, but works itself out in love. Even though we can't fall out of our justification, we may fall under our Father's displeasure because of our sin. But if we humble ourselves, confess our sins, plead for forgiveness, renew our faith, and repent, the light of God's face will once again shine on us.

Why We Believe It

The passages below inform the Christian doctrine of justification. God has spoken in the Bible, so we believe what he has said there. In the following pages, we'll explore this key doctrine and what it means for us as we follow Christ.

Blessed is the one whose transgression is forgiven,
    whose sin is covered.
Blessed is the man against whom the LORD counts no iniquity,
    and in whose spirit there is no deceit.
For when I kept silent, my bones wasted away
    through my groaning all day long.
For day and night your hand was heavy upon me;
    my strength was dried up as by the heat of summer.
I acknowledged my sin to you,
    and I did not cover my iniquity;
I said, "I will confess my transgressions to the LORD,"
    and you forgave the iniquity of my sin.

Psalm 32:1–5

But he was pierced for our transgressions;
    he was crushed for our iniquities;
upon him was the chastisement that brought us peace,
    and with his wounds we are healed.
All we like sheep have gone astray;
    we have turned—every one—to his own way;
and the LORD has laid on him
    the iniquity of us all.

Isaiah 53:5–6

But now the righteousness of God has been manifested apart from the law, although the Law and the Prophets bear witness to it—the righteousness of God through faith in Jesus Christ for all who believe. For there is no distinction: for all have sinned and fall short of the glory of God, and are justified by his grace as a gift, through the redemption that is in Christ Jesus, whom God put forward as a propitiation by his blood, to be received by faith. This was to show God's righteousness, because in his divine forbearance he had passed over former sins. It was to show his righteousness at the present time, so that he might be just and the justifier of the one who has faith in Jesus.

Then what becomes of our boasting? It is excluded. By what kind of law? By a law of works? No, but by the law of faith. For we hold that one is justified by faith apart from works of the law.

Romans 3:21–28

Indeed, I count everything as loss because of the surpassing worth of knowing Christ Jesus my Lord. For his sake I have suffered the loss of all things and count them as rubbish, in order that I may gain Christ and be found in him, not having a righteousness of my own that comes from the law, but that which comes through faith in Christ, the righteousness from God that depends on faith.

Philippians 3:8–9

How It Matters

 Throughout this chapter, we'll focus on the Bible's teaching about justification by faith. Because we're sinners who stand under the judgment of the holy God, we need a sacrifice to atone for all our sin. Jesus gave his life as the Lamb of God. This means that as Christians, our standing before God is no longer based on our own performance. Instead, we have been justified, declared righteous, because of Christ's performance. We are united to him; we are "in Christ." We are no longer aliens, no longer enemies, no longer condemned—but by grace, we are in Christ. We are the children of God. We're objects of the Father's love, justified, forgiven, righteous, eternally loved, and united to God and to one another.

1. The Need for Sacrifice

I spent one year in my personal devotions in the Pentateuch, the first five books of the Bible. It was a rich experience. Here's one thing I learned: You cannot see the brilliant glory of justification until you look at it through the lens of the Old Testament sacrificial system. Here's how.

In that system of regularly repeated sacrifices, you begin to see how seriously God takes sin. Every drop of animal blood was a reminder of the huge gap between the perfectly holy God and his consistently unholy people. The bloody, noisy slaughter of each animal confronted every Israelite with this truth: His or her sin caused that animal's death.

How in the world could the holy God have communion with unholy people? Would God bridge this huge, life-destroying sin gap, and if he would, how would he do it?

The answer is that sacrifices had to be made. These sacrifices had to satisfy the requirements of God's justice so he could extend the mercy of his forgiveness to sinners. The problem with the Old Testament sacrifices was that the satisfaction they supplied was sadly temporary.

Clearly a greater, final sacrifice was needed for the justification of sinners to be final and complete. A payment for sin needed to be made that would once and for all satisfy God's requirements and allow sinners to be forgiven and to live at peace with him.

This means that the entire old system, with all of its blood and gore, was a daily cry for the final Lamb of sacrifice, Jesus. He is our substitute. His substitutionary obedience and his substitutionary sacrifice mean that all who put their trust in him are fully and completely forgiven and able to stand before God as righteous.

This is what justification means. We are declared forgiven and righteous by God.

No sinner can earn, deserve, or achieve any of this on his own. Justification comes only through the righteous life and the acceptable death of Jesus. He is the only way by which justifying grace can flow to sinners like you and me.

Read: "But when Christ had offered for all time a single sacrifice for sins, he sat down at the right hand of God." HEBREWS 10:12

Reflect: As you think about what you've read, how do the Old Testament sacrifices make Jesus's death for sin more amazing and precious to you?

---

2. True Christianity

True Christian theology has a clear understanding of justification at its core. This truth separates Christianity from all other religions.

Think about false religions. They're all built on some form of the theology that the "gods" are upset with human beings. To make the gods happy, each person has to constantly work to calm their anger. You've got to obey all the rules or make repeated sacrifices. Each religion operates out of fear of divine anger. And all people are trapped—they can't escape having to obey the law perfectly.

But even people who aren't especially religious are still concerned with righteousness.

Everyone wants to be right. Everyone wants to think he has a good track record. People tend to want to be accepted because they are good. So your life is reduced to "Do right, good things happen. Do bad, bad things happen." Such a life is burdened by the constant need to perform, the constant need to measure up, and the constant need to convince yourself that you're good enough. What an exhausting way to live! And it never works.

The reality is that not only do we fall short of God's holy standards, but we also fall short of our standards for ourselves. Not only do we break God's rules, but we also consistently break our own rules.

This shows why justification is so precious. God declares us freely justified by forgiving our sins and by accepting us as righteous.

God does not justify us by declaring that our faith or our obedience count as righteousness. Instead, by grace, God justifies us by declaring that *Christ's* obedience and *his* payment for our sin count as ours.

There would be no such thing as Christianity if there were any way that a human being could stand righteous before God based on his own performance. If this were possible, the gospel would be a lie and the biblical story would not be needed.

This is true Christianity. We need to receive, accept, and rest in Christ and his righteousness as the sole means of our justification.

Read: "And to the one who does not work but believes in him who justifies the ungodly, his faith is counted as righteousness, just as David also speaks of the blessing of the one to whom God counts righteousness apart from works: 'Blessed are those whose lawless deeds are forgiven, and whose sins are covered; blessed is the man against whom the Lord will not count his sin.'" ROMANS 4:5-8

Reflect: Where do you feel as if you don't measure up? Why do you feel that way?

3. Good Enough?

You can't enter into the glorious rest of justification by hoping in yourself or your efforts. You'll never measure up to God's requirements.

Imagine a gym with a forty-foot-high ceiling. Imagine I entered the gym with the hope of standing in the middle of the gym floor and jumping up and touching the ceiling. You'd say, "That is insane. It'll never happen."

Then imagine further that you stand by the door and watch me begin to jump. You see the futility of what I am attempting. You feel sorry for me as I get more and more exhausted and further and further away from my goal. You begin to think, "This man needs to admit his inability and give up. Whatever hope is keeping him jumping—that is false hope."

So it is with justification. The doorway to the warehouse of God's justifying mercies is *hopelessness*.

You have to abandon hope in yourself in order to run in the hope of God. This hopelessness leads you to God's mercy seat, where eternal, secure, and unshakable hope is found.

This is not hope you have earned, but hope that has been earned by another and given to you by grace.

The bad news about yourself points to the good news. This is the gospel. And it's the most essential and glorious message ever written and spoken. In his righteous life and substitutionary death, Jesus has made it possible for us to be forgiven, accepted, and declared righteous by God. This is the ultimate good news.

Read: "For by grace you have been saved through faith. And this is not your own doing; it is the gift of God, not a result of works, so that no one may boast." EPHESIANS 2:8–9

Reflect: How is "admitting your inability" so wildly different from what culture tells everyone today? Why does culture's confidence in human ability ultimately lead to hopelessness?

4. Two Huge Tiny Words

Justification focuses on our legal standing before God. We are declared righteous! However, there's more. Justification is also about a brand-new identity. We are God's children!

This new identity can be summarized in two of the most important words in the Bible: *in Christ*.

These two words point to a Bible truth that's called "union with Christ." This truth, that by grace we have been united to Christ, is a dominant theme in the apostle Paul's writing.

In the New Testament, Paul uses the phrase "in Christ" dozens of times. Additionally, he says that we were chosen "*in him* before the foundation of the world" (Eph. 1:4). By God's sovereign redemptive purpose, we were united to Christ before we took our first breaths. This is an amazing thing to consider. It was not that we got smart and found Christ. No, God placed us in Christ as a sovereign decision of his redeeming grace.

It's impossible to really understand the truth of justification without understanding union with Christ. All of the graces of the gospel flow to us because we are in Christ:

- We are justified because we are in Christ.
- We are being sanctified because we are in Christ.
- We are loved as adopted children because we are in Christ.
- We are forgiven because we are in Christ.
- We have every need supplied because we are in Christ.
- We are objects of the Father's love because we are in Christ.
- We have eternal hope because we are in Christ.

Here's what one Bible teacher has said about the blessings of being in Christ: "Union with Christ is the fountainhead from which flows the Christian's every spiritual blessing—repentance and faith, pardon, justification, adoption, sanctification, perseverance, and glorification" (Robert L. Reymond, *A New Systematic Theology of the Christian Faith*, 2nd ed. [Thomas Nelson, 2010], 759).

Justification means we are no longer enemies of God. Now we are his children. Being in Christ means God is for us. And if God is for us, who can stand against us?

Read: "And because of him you are in Christ Jesus, who became to us wisdom from God, righteousness and sanctification and redemption, so that, as it is written, 'Let the one who boasts, boast in the Lord.'"
1 CORINTHIANS 1:30–31

Reflect: If God declares you righteous because you are in Christ, what does that say about how secure your justification is?

5. New Life, New Living

One of the most encouraging passages in the New Testament is Galatians 2:20. Take a moment to read the full verse, included below.

Notice two statements in this verse that apply to all believers. The first is a statement of *historical gospel fact*: "I have been crucified with Christ." We are united with Christ in his death and resurrection.

This means that when Christ died, we died. And when Christ rose, we, too, rose to newness of life. Jesus didn't die so there might be a *chance* that we might be saved. No, when he went to the cross, he took with him the names of all who were united to him. His payment for sin was our payment. Why? Because of this historical fact: We were united with him when he suffered and died on the cross.

The fact of our union with Christ means something more. Galatians 2:20 also contains a statement of *present gospel reality*: "It is no longer I who live, but Christ who lives in me." Because we are united to him, he empowers us to do what we could never have done before.

Clearly Paul is not saying that he is physically dead. If he were, he couldn't have written the book of Galatians. Instead, Paul is saying that because of our union with Christ, we experience new life. This life, which ignites new thoughts, desires, and actions, is not ours. It's Christ's.

This means that the gospel is not a system of self-reformation. In order to truly change, we need more than a commitment to self-discipline.

Instead, being in Christ means that the power of the resurrection is now the power that animates our living. This is another provision of God's grace. Sin doesn't just leave us condemned. It also renders us unable both to be what God has designed us to be and also to do what God has commanded us to do. Yet in Christ we are empowered for a brand-new way of living.

Read: "I have been crucified with Christ. It is no longer I who live, but Christ who lives in me. And the life I now live in the flesh I live by faith in the Son of God, who loved me and gave himself for me." GALATIANS 2:20

Reflect: Where are you giving in to thoughts, desires, and temptations that you now have the power to resist? Where in your life do you need to exercise your power to live in a new way?

6. One Big Family

In Christ, we now are accepted as the adopted sons and daughters of the Most High God.

It would still be amazing grace even if God canceled our condemnation but kept himself separate from us. It would be wonderful mercy if he simply tolerated us. But only lavish grace could take rebel enemies and welcome them as dearly loved children. In Christ, we now live with all the rights and privileges of children of the almighty one.

Where does this love come from? The incalculable love that the Father has for the Son now flows to us as his adopted children. Why? Because we are one with Christ.

And this unity with Christ is also the foundation of our own love. In Christ, we have a new culture of love and unity with one another. In his prayer for his disciples, and for us, Jesus makes this clear:

> I do not ask for these only, but also for those who will believe in me through their word, that they may all be one, just as you, Father, are in me, and I in you, that they also may be in us, so that the world may believe that you have sent me. The glory that you have given me I have given to them, that they may be one even as we are one, I in them and you in me, that they may become perfectly one, so that the world may know that you sent me and loved them even as you loved me. (John 17:20–23)

We could never create this unity on our own. We are one because we are one *in Christ*. We are in him, and he is in us. And because this is true of you and me, we are united to one another as well.

Being in Christ is the unique foundation that unites all who have faith in him. It is a unity that spans race, social class, gender, ethnicity, and geography.

Read: "See what kind of love the Father has given to us, that we should be called children of God; and so we are." 1 JOHN 3:1

Reflect: What causes you to not feel like a beloved child of God? Why? And how is your adoption in Christ greater than those feelings?

---

7. New Life in Christ

The doctrines of justification and union with Christ are the best pieces of news sinners in this sin-scarred world could ever hear. What we never could have dreamed has become ours. And what we have no capacity to earn is now ours in Christ.

God uses these realities to change us. Through uniting us to Christ, he changes how we think, what we desire, and how we live. Here are five words that capture the new lifestyle that is propelled by the doctrine of God's justifying grace.

Humility. The doctrine of justification confronts me and you with how messed up we are—and the fact that we can't do anything to restore ourselves. The proper response is humility. Humility is one of the doctrine of justification's good fruits.

Gratitude. Because sin is self-centered, complaint is more natural for us than gratitude. Here again, a beautiful fruit of justification is a profound sense of gratitude. You can't properly reflect on the doctrine of justification without a heart overflowing with thankfulness. Gone are the days of "I earned it, I deserve it, so I will boast about it."

Freedom. Justification by grace through faith really does set you free. The justifying mercies of Christ release you from the requirements of the law and from the paralyzing burden of guilt and shame. We don't have to go slump-backed through life, protecting ourselves from onlookers as if we are rejected, unwanted, and unworthy. We are children of the King, his door is open, and we are welcomed.

Values. I can lose sight of what is truly important. One of the benefits of God's justifying mercies is their power to clarify and reorient our values. Think of what God did in order to deliver his justifying grace to you. Could there possibly be any treasure of more value than this?

Defense. It's true that justifying grace has given us peace with God. Yet spiritual war rages all around us. Even the most mundane moments are complicated by this spiritual war. But the doctrine of justification tells you that your acceptance with God has not been and never will be based on the track record of your righteousness. So whenever Satan throws your unrighteousness at you, throw the perfect righteousness of Jesus back at him, and he will flee.

Read: "What then shall we say to these things? If God is for us, who can be against us? He who did not spare his own Son but gave him up for us all, how will he not also with him graciously give us all things?" ROMANS 8:31–32

Reflect: How has justifying grace transformed your heart and the way you respond in the situations, locations, and relationships of your daily life?

10

Sanctification

What We Believe

The people God has justified (declared righteous) he also sanctifies (enables to live righteously). He does this both through the death and resurrection of Jesus Christ, and also by his word and Spirit living in believers. For them, the rule of sin is destroyed, and they are more and more strengthened by grace to pursue holiness and resist sinful desires. Yet the corruption of sin remains in every part of them. There is an ongoing war between sinful desires and Spirit-led desires. In this war, the remaining influence of sin may prevail for a time. Yet through the continual strength of the Spirit of Christ, Christians' new nature will overcome. As a result, they will grow in grace and holiness.

Why We Believe It

The passages below inform the Christian doctrine of sanctification. God has spoken in the Bible, so we believe what he has said there. In the following pages, we'll explore this key doctrine and what it means for us as we follow Christ.

I am speaking in human terms, because of your natural limitations. For just as you once presented your members as slaves to impurity and to lawlessness leading to more lawlessness, so now present your members as slaves to righteousness leading to sanctification.

Romans 6:19

For this reason I bow my knees before the Father, from whom every family in heaven and on earth is named, that according to the riches of his glory he may grant you to be strengthened with power through his Spirit in your inner being, so that Christ may dwell in your hearts through faith—that you, being rooted and grounded in love, may have strength to comprehend with all the saints what is the breadth and length and height and depth, and to know the love of Christ that surpasses knowledge, that you may be filled with all the fullness of God.

Ephesians 3:14–19

Speaking the truth in love, we are to grow up in every way into him who is the head, into Christ, from whom the whole body, joined and held together by every joint with which it is equipped, when each part is working properly, makes the body grow so that it builds itself up in love.

Ephesians 4:15–16

Strive for peace with everyone, and for the holiness without which no one will see the Lord.

Hebrews 12:14

Beloved, I urge you as sojourners and exiles to abstain from the passions of the flesh, which wage war against your soul.

1 Peter 2:11

How It Matters

 Throughout this chapter, we'll focus on the Bible's teaching about sanctification. In justification, God declares us righteous in Christ, and in sanctification, he begins to actually change us into what he's declared us to be. It's a continuation of God's work of redemption in our lives. Like a master artist, God is shaping us to be more like Jesus. God uses various tools in sanctifying us. He uses our actions as we pursue holiness. He uses our prayerful time in his word. He uses other members of the body of Christ, the church. And he even uses the fires of suffering and hardship to purify our lives and refine our hearts. Yet no change, no growth, and no transformation can happen without the gracious work of God's Holy Spirit.

1. What Is Sanctification?

I remember vividly the night, when I was a little boy, that conviction of sin and saving grace exploded into my heart. I confessed my sin and pleaded for the Redeemer's forgiveness. It was a heart-gripping, life-changing moment of spiritual rescue. It was the beginning of the journey of grace that I am still on.

As stunning as the first moment of redeeming rescue was, it was just the start of a lifelong process of redeeming grace. God is not satisfied to just declare us righteous. This God of mercy wants more for us. He will not rest until he has actually formed true righteousness in us. The process by which he does this work in us is called sanctification. *So sanctification is the process by which God actually makes us what he has declared us to be in Christ: righteous.* This means our Savior is still at work saving us.

Sanctification is not rescuing us from external evil, with all of its temptations. Although we have been forgiven, declared righteous, and adopted as God's children, the muck and mess of sin still remain in us. That means the primary focus of sanctification is the ongoing, lifelong rescue of us *from us*.

So the doctrine of sanctification requires you to admit that you are deeply in need of God's help. And it requires you to accept that no matter how much you have grown in grace, you still need to grow in grace. There simply is no such thing as a sanctification graduate.

And even though God's truth is a powerful tool, our sanctification is not primarily about acquiring information. You can be theologically smart and biblically literate and still be spiritually immature. Sanctification is about heart and life transformation. It is about character formation. It is about being molded, by the power of God's saving hand, into the likeness of Jesus Christ.

You will look the same, your natural gifts will remain the same, and your basic personality will still be in place after years of sanctifying grace has done its wonderful work in you. Yet you will not be the same. Why? Because you will look more like Jesus than you did when you first believed.

Read: "And now I commend you to God and to the word of his grace, which is able to build you up and to give you the inheritance among all those who are sanctified." ACTS 20:32

Reflect: How is the concept of sanctification different than you might have imagined when you were younger?

---

2. God Works to Make You More Like Jesus

I was in Asia visiting an art museum, as I often do when I travel. I walked around a corner and into a gallery that held a mesmerizing collection of paintings. From a distance, each painting looked like undulating waves of gray on a pure white canvas. The waves had the illusion of being in motion, and while the wave pattern on each painting was unique, each one shared the singular beauty of design. You knew right away that these stunning works of art had all come from the same creator.

After a few minutes of observation from a distance, I picked out one of the paintings that seemed especially interesting and walked over to see it up close. When I got within inches of that canvas, I was blown away by what I saw. It was covered in handwritten, numerically sequenced sets of numbers. There were thousands and thousands of numbers in hundreds and hundreds of rolls. The waves were created by how darkly the artist wrote each number on the canvas and how closely he placed each number to the next. The concept was mind-boggling, the composition was intricate and complex, the execution was exquisite, and the overall effect was beautiful.

That the artist had taken something so mundane as rows of little numbers and employed them to create such wonder almost brought me to tears. I thought of the brilliance of the artist. I thought about the commitment it took to complete this process. And then I thought of how satisfying it must have been for the artist to walk into that gallery and see the beauty that he alone had created.

Far more than those amazing paintings, our sanctification is the detailed work of a perfectly committed divine artist.

In the small moments and grand dramas of our lives, an artist is at work. He's creating the most beautiful image ever—the image of the Son of God. We are the canvas. In the tiniest of increments, day after day after day, God transforms us. He's changing us from the ugly messes we were in our sin to the beautiful sons and daughters he saved us to be.

Although God calls you to give yourself to the labor of your own spirituality, sanctification is *his* work. He never gets bored, he never grows weary, he never is frustrated, and his commitment to complete his redemptive artwork never fades.

There will be a day when we will walk into the greatest gallery ever to see the most detailed and beautiful work ever, finally complete, and we'll spend the rest of eternity in wonder and celebration.

Read: "Therefore, my beloved, as you have always obeyed, so now, not only as in my presence but much more in my absence, work out your own salvation with fear and trembling, for it is God who works in you, both to will and to work for his good pleasure." PHILIPPIANS 2:12–13

Reflect: In what small ways (or big ways) have you seen God change and transform your life?

3. God Uses Your Activity to Make You More Like Jesus

Imagine that you are given a brand-new home that is beautiful in every way. Imagine your excitement as you open the door and walk from beautiful room to beautiful room. Now imagine that for all of its beauty, there is a grave problem: An evil and deceitful killer lives there. However harmless he may seem at times, he is out for one thing: to do you harm. He wants to rob you of your joy, destroy your trust in your benefactor, and fill you with fear. There is no good in him, his intentions are always evil, and he must never be trusted. Will you ever consider finding a way to make it work for him to live there? Will you not do everything you can to rid yourself of his evil presence?

So it is with the sin that remains in us. Sin is a deceitful, malevolent, and seductive killer, still lurking in the corners of your heart. Sin is always harmful, always destructive, and never good. Sin is not something that you should try to find a way to live with. It must be destroyed. It must be put to death. The goal of God's sanctifying grace is the final death of the sin that remains in us.

How do we do this? I love Paul's words in 2 Corinthians 10:4–5: "For the weapons of our warfare are not of the flesh but have divine power to destroy strongholds. We destroy arguments and every lofty opinion raised against the knowledge of God, and take every thought captive to obey Christ."

Any thing, thought, desire, motivation, purpose, plan, attitude, or action that in any way, shape, or form opposes the knowledge of God and new life in his Son must be destroyed. How? By the truth of God in his word, by humble and honest confession, and by seeking the Spirit's help. Through his grace, we are enabled to turn away from everything that opposes God and his will.

We do not have the power to kill sin on our own, but with confidence in the Spirit's presence and work, we take up weapons that have divine power and go about the work of hunting it down and killing it (Col. 3:1–4). May God give us the grace we need to live in step with the Spirit.

Read: "What shall we say then? Are we to continue in sin that grace may abound? By no means! How can we who died to sin still live in it?" ROMANS 6:1–2

Reflect: When does your faith seem most vibrant—during two hours each Sunday or during the week when fighting temptation? Why?

4. God Uses His Word to Make You More Like Jesus

In the over four decades that I have been in ministry, I have spent thousands of hours counseling troubled, depressed, fearful, angry, hurting, beaten-down, and confused Christians. It has not been a burden but a huge personal blessing. Not every ending was a happy one. Yet I am thankful that I have seen fresh starts, new hope, and new beginnings over and over again.

One troubling theme that popped up again and again was how few of them had regular habits of personal study, worship, and prayer. Because of the absence of these regular habits, many of my counselees lacked personal growth. And they weren't prepared for the troubles of life.

Spending time each day in the Bible and prayer is a powerful tool of sanctifying grace in the hands of our Redeemer. Permit me to list ways in which the regular habit of personal worship contributes to God's ongoing work of personal heart and life transformation. Daily study of God's word, worship, and prayer will result in the following:

- a deeper knowledge of the nature and character of God
- a clearer understanding of how God works
- an ever-deepening love for and trust in him
- a deeper willingness and commitment to surrender your life to him
- a deeper knowledge of yourself as sinner, sufferer, and saint
- a deeper and more practical grasp of the truths of God's word
- a clearer and more practical understanding of the gospel of Jesus Christ
- a deeper awareness of the nature of sin and temptation
- more regular patterns of conviction of sin, confession, and repentance
- better preparation for spiritual warfare and Satan's attacks

Are you committed to giving yourself to God's purposes of personal transformation? If so, then you will see the discipline of personal study, worship, and prayer not as a spiritual burden but as a loving welcome.

Here I am welcomed to sit at the feet of my Father, to experience his love once again, and to take in his wisdom again. Here I am welcomed to look at myself in the perfect mirror of Scripture, seeing myself with clarity and accuracy. Here I am encouraged, comforted, and strengthened. And here I am given reasons to face my day with faith, hope, and courage.

The word is an essential tool of God's sanctifying grace. Being invited to commune daily with God is not only a tool of his sanctifying grace but also a sign of your Savior's love for you.

Read: "Since we have these promises, beloved, let us cleanse ourselves from every defilement of body and spirit, bringing holiness to completion in the fear of God." 2 CORINTHIANS 7:1

Reflect: How would you rate your commitment to daily connection and fellowship with Jesus in his word? What part of your daily routine can you change to enjoy his welcome more deeply?

5. God Uses the Church to Make You More Like Jesus

The ministry of the church is an important tool in the hands of the Redeemer. It's another way that he advances the saving work he has begun in us. There is no such thing as a vibrant and ever-maturing Christian life without the ministry of the local church.

For the believer, the church exists because the lifelong process of progressive sanctification exists. The apostle Paul clearly captures for us the essential sanctifying ministry of the body of Christ (Eph. 4:11–16).

Think of how every ministry of the body of Christ contributes to the process of your spiritual growth. We need to participate in public worship. We need to sing the truths of the gospel not only into our own hearts but into the ears and hearts of one another. We need the public reading and teaching of God's word, always being reminded of its authority, sufficiency, and life-giving wisdom. We need the mutual-ministry fellowship and self-sacrificing love of the body of Christ. We need the example, wisdom, rebuke, and encouragement of mature brothers and sisters who understand how to live as children of God in this fallen world.

So if you take your ongoing sanctification seriously, don't just be thankful for your church. And don't just be a casual attender. Instead, joyfully participate in all of its public and private ministries.

The importance of the church in God's work of growing us in grace is stated clearly and powerfully by Paul in 1 Timothy 3. The church is the pillar and foundation of the truth by which God sanctifies us. That means that there is no growth in grace without the impact of the church on our hearts.

Read: "I hope to come to you soon, but I am writing these things to you so that, if I delay, you may know how one ought to behave in the household of God, which is the church of the living God, a pillar and buttress of the truth." 1 TIMOTHY 3:14–15

Reflect: When you go to church, how do you seek out ways to help others grow and become more like Christ?

---

6. God Uses Hardship to Make You More Like Jesus

You have probably never heard anyone say, "I had three of the easiest years of my life . . . and I learned and changed so much."

The Bible regularly confronts us with the fact that God uses things we'd like to avoid in order to produce good in us. But we struggle to see difficulty, in the hands of God, as a tool for massive spiritual good.

I imagine that you, like me, tend to think that a good life is a comfortable life. We get irritated, impatient, and angry at even minor difficulties. Long lines make us mad. Having to listen to an overtalkative person makes us impatient. A day when we don't feel great causes us to grumble.

Is it any wonder, then, that we have a hard time being thankful that the difficulties in our lives are a primary tool of God's transforming grace? As long as self is in the center, we will struggle with anything that is uncomfortable.

So when it comes to the sanctifying power of difficulty in the hands of God, we need to do two things.

First, we need to humbly *confess* that we often treasure our comfort more than we treasure sanctifying grace. We cannot long for redeeming grace and curse difficulty at the same time. That's like hiring someone to build you a house and then requiring him to leave his tools at home.

Second, we need to *remember* the cross of Jesus, which shows that God brings rich, beautiful, and eternal spiritual good out of bad things. From the very bad moment of Christ's crucifixion, plotted and executed by evil men, grace upon grace flows to all who believe.

Suffering will enter our doors. But these hard moments will never be a sign that God has forsaken us; rather, they will be an indication that his transforming grace is at work. For this reason, we can look difficulty in the face and be thankful, not for the pain of the difficulty but for what God will produce in us and through us by it.

Read: "Count it all joy, my brothers, when you meet trials of various kinds, for you know that the testing of your faith produces steadfastness. And let steadfastness have its full effect, that you may be perfect and complete, lacking in nothing." JAMES 1:2–4

Reflect: Stop reading for a moment and humbly confess your love of what is comfortable, and then pray for the grace to love God and his redeeming work more.

---

7. God Uses the Holy Spirit to Make You More Like Jesus

God uses many tools of sanctification to continue his redeeming work in our hearts. Yet none of these tools has magical sanctifying power. A hammer in a carpenter's hand has no power in itself. Its ability to drive a nail into a piece of wood is entirely dependent on the carpenter who holds it. So it is with all the tools that God uses to grow us in his grace. Those tools have no power on their own apart from the powerful work of the Holy Spirit, who uses them to change our hearts and lives.

The Holy Spirit works to grow us in grace in the following ways.

The Spirit blesses us with his ministry of the conviction of sin. There would be no grace of sanctification without the grace of conviction (John 16:8). Conviction of sin is not judgment. Instead, it is the work of our loving heavenly Father. Through the heart-softening work of the Holy Spirit, he draws us near so we walk closer and closer to him.

The Spirit illumines God's word for us. Jesus said to his confused and fearful disciples, "When the Spirit of truth comes, he will guide you into all the truth" (John 16:13). As we commit to the study of Scripture, the Holy Spirit works to illumine our minds and enliven our hearts. As a result, we are not just informed by what we have studied but transformed by it as well.

The Spirit empowers us to obey. Because sin leaves us unable (as well as unwilling) to heed God's commands, we desperately need empowering grace. That grace comes to us in the person and work of the Holy Spirit (Eph. 1:17–19). He lives inside of us, empowering us to take new steps of faith and obedience. He helps us gain new ground in our growth in grace.

The Spirit carries our cries to the Father. In the middle of our sanctification, sometimes we don't know how to pray, but we do not need to be discouraged. The Holy Spirit helps us (Rom. 8:26). He prays for us and carries our messy, confused groanings to the Father.

Be thankful today for the Holy Spirit's presence and power in your life. Be thankful that because he is in you, for you, and with you, you will continue to grow in grace.

Read: "Likewise the Spirit helps us in our weakness. For we do not know what to pray for as we ought, but the Spirit himself intercedes for us with groanings too deep for words." ROMANS 8:26

Reflect: Where has the Holy Spirit recently convicted you of sin? How did you respond? Why?

11

Perseverance and Glorification

What We Believe

True Christians will not finally fall away from grace. Instead, they'll persevere in that grace and be eternally saved. The perseverance of the saints does not depend on their own free will, but on the choice of God's free, unchangeable, and redemptive love. However, Christians may fall into sins and incur God's displeasure, grieve the Holy Spirit, hurt others, and bring temporary judgment on themselves. After death, people's bodies decay and return to dust, but their souls live forever. The souls of righteous people will be made perfectly holy. And in heaven, they will behold the face of God in light and glory, waiting for the full redemption of their bodies.

Why We Believe It

The passages below inform the Christian doctrines of perseverance and glorification. God has spoken in the Bible, so we believe what he has said there. In the following pages, we'll explore these key doctrines and what they mean for us as we follow Christ.

For we know that if the tent that is our earthly home is destroyed, we have a building from God, a house not made with hands, eternal in the heavens. For in this tent we groan, longing to put on our heavenly dwelling, if indeed by putting it on we may not be found naked. For while we are still in this tent, we groan, being burdened—not that we would be unclothed, but that we would be further clothed, so that what is mortal may be swallowed up by life. He who has prepared us for this very thing is God, who has given us the Spirit as a guarantee.

So we are always of good courage. We know that while we are at home in the body we are away from the Lord, for we walk by faith, not by sight. Yes, we are of good courage, and we would rather be away from the body and at home with the Lord.

2 Corinthians 5:1–8

To this he called you through our gospel, so that you may obtain the glory of our Lord Jesus Christ.

2 Thessalonians 2:14

Therefore I endure everything for the sake of the elect, that they also may obtain the salvation that is in Christ Jesus with eternal glory. The saying is trustworthy, for:

If we have died with him, we will also live with him;
   if we endure, we will also reign with him;
if we deny him, he also will deny us;
   if we are faithless, he remains faithful—

for he cannot deny himself.

2 Timothy 2:10–13

Blessed be the God and Father of our Lord Jesus Christ! According to his great mercy, he has caused us to be born again to a living hope through the resurrection of Jesus Christ from the dead, to an inheritance that is imperishable, undefiled, and unfading, kept in heaven for you, who by God's power are being guarded through faith for a salvation ready to be revealed in the last time.

1 Peter 1:3–5

See what kind of love the Father has given to us, that we should be called children of God; and so we are. The reason why the world does not know us is that it did not know him. Beloved, we are God's children now, and what we will be has not yet appeared; but we know that when he appears we shall be like him, because we shall see him as he is. And everyone who thus hopes in him purifies himself as he is pure.

Everyone who makes a practice of sinning also practices lawlessness; sin is lawlessness. You know that he appeared in order to take away sins, and in him there is no sin. No one who abides in him keeps on sinning; no one who keeps on sinning has either seen him or known him. Little children, let no one deceive you. Whoever practices righteousness is righteous, as he is righteous. Whoever makes a practice of sinning is of the devil, for the devil has been sinning from the beginning. The reason the Son of God appeared was to destroy the works of the devil. No one born of God makes a practice of sinning, for God's seed abides in him; and he cannot keep on sinning, because he has been born of God. By this it is evident who are the children of God, and who are the children of the devil: whoever does not practice righteousness is not of God, nor is the one who does not love his brother.

1 John 3:1–10

How It Matters

Throughout this chapter, we'll focus on the Bible's teaching about persevering in this life until we enjoy the glory of the next life. Until then, our loving God protects us, just as a shepherd guards his sheep. In his extraordinary power, he keeps us, often using ordinary disciplines of grace and active faith. He also sustains our faith by firing our imagination with the glory that awaits us. We persevere as we behold our promised future by faith. It's often hard to even imagine, because that glory is so perfectly flawless. Yet one day, every believer in Jesus will be like him. We'll rejoice at the funeral of sin and all its effects. And until then, the promise of future glorification is our motivation in the present. We persevere as we look to the glory Christ has promised to his own.

1. Protected by God's Love

To unpack the doctrine of perseverance is really to meditate on the nature, the work, and the power of the love of God. It is the power of love that protects us. It is not *our* love for God that keeps us to the end, but *God's* unshakable love for his own. Romans 8:28–39 is incredibly helpful here.

God's redeeming work in the hearts and lives of his children is unstoppable. Romans 8:29–30 is an airtight passage: "Those whom he foreknew he also predestined. . . . Those whom he predestined he also called, and those whom he called he also justified, and those whom he justified he also glorified." By this unbreakable chain of grace, God will complete his work in the life of every person who has placed his or her trust in Jesus.

God exercises his sovereignty for the redemptive good of his children. "All things work together for good, for those who are called according to his purpose" (Rom. 8:28). The one who is in control of everything is right now exercising that control. Why? For the redemptive good of his people.

Along the way, God will supply everything his children need. Since what Paul has just written in Romans 8:28–30 is true, he asks these rhetorical questions: "If God is for us, who can be against us? He who did not spare his own Son, . . . how will he not also with him graciously give us all things?" (8:31–32). If God spared nothing to bring us to himself, does it make any sense at all to think that he would abandon us between our justification and our glorification?

Nothing can separate God's children from his love. Here is the final argument Paul makes for the perseverance of the saints. Yes, they suffer in this groaning world; yes, there are times they don't even know how to pray; yes, they live with the condemning attacks of the enemy; and yes, they wander and stray. Yet nothing in heaven or on earth can ever separate them from the love of God in Christ Jesus (Rom. 8:35–39). He doesn't love you because you believe. No, you believe because he loved and is loving you. We are secure in his love.

Read: "I will make with them an everlasting covenant, that I will not turn away from doing good to them. And I will put the fear of me in their hearts, that they may not turn from me." JEREMIAH 32:40

Reflect: Where do you most often look to find and feel God's love for you? How is the sacrifice of Jesus the best place to discover God's love?

---

2. Kept by the Good Shepherd

The power that keeps us is the power of the Lord, our shepherd. Our salvation is initiated by him, continued by him, and finalized by him.

If the stability and continuance of our salvation were resting on *our* shoulders, then the Christian life would be scary, fearful, and full of anxiety. With sin still inside us, we would always be trying to earn and secure our place and never quite sure that we had. But we can rest because the good shepherd will keep every one of his sheep forever:

All that the Father gives me will come to me, and whoever comes to me I will never cast out. For I have come down from heaven, not to do my own will but the will of him who sent me. And this is the will of him who sent me, that I should lose nothing of all that he has given me, but raise it up on the last day. For this is the will of my Father, that everyone who looks on the Son and believes in him should have eternal life, and I will raise him up on the last day. (John 6:37–40)

This should be an enormous encouragement to any Christian who is struggling with the hardships and temptations of this fallen world. There is no metaphor or mystery to Jesus's words. They are direct, and their meaning is clear.

First Jesus says, "It's the Father who gives you to me, and whomever the Father gives to me, I will never cast out." You and I come to Christ because of the Father's initiative. And we are kept by the Savior's will and power. God draws us; God protects us.

Then Jesus doubles down on his declaration: "I will lose nothing of what the Father has given me; so those who believe in me, I will raise up on the last day." And later he says, "No one is able to snatch them out of the Father's hand" (John 10:29). This is where our hope rests. We do not have the independent spiritual power to keep ourselves to the end. God really is our refuge and strength.

Why do you and I persevere? Because we are held, by grace, in the Father's safe and sovereign hand.

Read: "My sheep hear my voice, and I know them, and they follow me. I give them eternal life, and they will never perish, and no one will snatch them out of my hand. My Father, who has given them to me, is greater than all, and no one is able to snatch them out of the Father's hand. I and the Father are one." JOHN 10:27-30

Reflect: Would you rather have the safety of your eternal soul protected by your own strength or by God's? Why?

3. Kept by Active Faith

Since the good shepherd keeps us, does it make any difference how we live? Is casual, lazy, and consumerist Christianity okay? If we're this secure, why not enjoy the pleasures of sin for a bit?

The Bible tells us that God exercises his protecting power through the vehicle of regular means:

- You are not kept because you have regular personal worship, but your Savior employs that regular habit to keep you.
- You are not kept because you are faithful in participating in the gathering of your church for public worship and teaching, but God uses that commitment to keep you.
- You are not kept because you commit yourself every day to live inside of the boundaries of God's commands, but God uses that discipline to keep you.

How does God do the extraordinary work of keeping you until the end? He works through ordinary means. He uses the regular habits of the Christian life. Consider the following passages from God's word.

Do you not know that in a race all the runners run, but only one receives the prize? So run that you may obtain it. (1 Cor. 9:24)

Let us not grow weary of doing good, for in due season we will reap, if we do not give up. (Gal. 6:9)

You have need of endurance, so that when you have done the will of God you may receive what is promised. (Heb. 10:36)

I am coming soon. Hold fast what you have, so that no one may seize your crown. (Rev. 3:11)

So you work, you fight, you resist, you obey, you confess, you repent, you worship, and you study. And you do it all over and over again. None of these disciplines would be enough to keep you forever in the shepherd's fold. However, each is a tool the Father uses to keep us to the end.

The God who goes to extraordinary lengths to protect his children uses ordinary means to do so. So we make those means the constant habits of our lives.

No, the doctrine of perseverance doesn't teach us that the way we live doesn't make any difference. It calls us to the very opposite.

Read: "Therefore, since we are surrounded by so great a cloud of witnesses, let us also lay aside every weight, and sin which clings so closely, and let us run with endurance the race that is set before us." HEBREWS 12:1

Reflect: What was most difficult (and most clarifying) about today's reading? How would you explain this to someone younger than you?

4. More Than We Can Imagine

Your ability to imagine is an important part of your faith. Let me explain. For the believer, imagination is not the ability to conjure up what is unreal. Instead, it's the ability to see what is real but unseen.

We are called to "see" God's saving grace, Christ's cleansing blood, and the Holy Spirit living inside of us. We live with the "sight" of the storehouse of blessings that are ours as the children of God. We "behold" the magnificent and glorious future that is ours by grace. God, in mercy, gives us eyes to "see" what sin normally blinds us from seeing.

Imagination is a vital part of his gift of faith to us.

So imagine with me being given a gift that can never be taken away. This gift will never grow old, wear out, break, stop functioning, or lose its value.

We are used to things decaying. Our physical bodies eventually grow weak, frail, and old. The new car, which even smelled new, soon becomes the used car that you're thinking of trading in for a newer model. Similarly, the most amazing athlete doesn't stay amazing forever. Our relationships don't last eternally. You'll outlive the puppy you just brought home. And the blossoms in your garden will turn brown and fall to the ground. We are so familiar with so many things fading away in our lives.

That makes it hard for us to imagine a gift that will never fade but only become more beautiful. It's hard for us to imagine a gift that doesn't disappoint as the years go on, but rather fulfills its promise to bless us with matchless glory.

It's hard for us to grasp with our imaginations what saving grace is able to do. Why? Because this gift is unlike anything we have ever experienced in our lives.

There is glory coming that's beyond any glory we have ever imagined.

Read: "But we impart a secret and hidden wisdom of God, which God decreed before the ages for our glory. None of the rulers of this age understood this, for if they had, they would not have crucified the Lord of glory. But, as it is written, 'What no eye has seen, nor ear heard, nor the heart of man imagined, what God has prepared for those who love him.'" 1 CORINTHIANS 2:7–9

Reflect: What aspect of the future glory of God's promised grace truly fills you with wonder and excitement? Why?

---

5. Flawless Future

God will complete his work in us. One day, we will be finally and fully redeemed. We will be made in the likeness of our Savior in every way.

The great celestial orchestra will be in full crescendo as the fully glorified children of God march into their final home. They will receive crowns. Yet all the praise, worship, and celebration will be directed at their Savior as they begin to sing glory songs to him that will never end.

It is hard to wrap our limited little brains around what glorification actually means.

We have spent our lives around flawed people. Even the most mature and noble among us have their nobility nicked, scratched, and dented by sin. From birth to death, flawed is our everyday normal. Flawed thoughts, flawed desires, flawed attitudes, flawed words, flawed actions and reactions, flawed decisions, flawed love, flawed relationships, flawed worship—this is the human community we are accustomed to.

Only as we observe Jesus during his brief journey on earth do we get a glimpse of what our flawless future will look like. The incarnated and then resurrected Jesus is the clearest promise of our future glorification.

So God calls us to hold on to this promise: that he will complete what he has begun. In the meantime, he blesses us with the grace to hold on to the promise that we will be like him. With expectancy tempered by patience, we don't stop looking to Jesus.

There is no better single-phrase summary of what glorification means than these five words: "We shall be like him" (1 John 3:2).

All of God's grace-adopted children will finally be like Jesus:

- That flawed husband, struggling with anger, will be like him.
- That young person, fighting temptation at her school, will be like him.
- That disgruntled student athlete will be like him.
- That guy yelling at traffic will be like him.
- That person, crippled by anxiety, will be like him.

Because all of these people are true children of God, their futures are bright. What a stunning hope to hold on to.

It's hard to live in the middle, with all of its struggle and disappointments. That's why it's important to hold on to the guarantee of our glorification. Live now among the flaws with future flawlessness in view.

Read: "Beloved, we are God's children now, and what we will be has not yet appeared; but we know that when he appears we shall be like him, because we shall see him as he is." 1 JOHN 3:2

Reflect: Which one of the bullet points above resonated most with you? Why?

---

6. The Best Funeral

We all hate funerals because they confront us with death and final separation. Yet there is one funeral to look forward to and celebrate. One day sin will die. Glorification means the final funeral of sin.

Imagine being finally free of sin's burden and bondage. Its corrupting power will die. Imagine life without daily spiritual warfare. Imagine the final defeat of the devil and all the forces of darkness. It seems too good to imagine, but that day is coming; the death and resurrection of Jesus Christ is our guarantee. Consider the words of Revelation 22:3: "No longer will there be anything accursed, but the throne of God and of the Lamb will be in it, and his servants will worship him."

When Revelation says "no longer will there be anything accursed," you know that sin has finally and forever been removed. And as the glorified children of God, we will sing these words with joy unlike anything we have experienced before:

"O death, where is your victory?
O death, where is your sting?"

The sting of death is sin, and the power of sin is the law. But thanks be to God, who gives us the victory through our Lord Jesus Christ. (1 Cor. 15:55–57)

So as we live in this world where sin still does its ugly work, we refuse to give up hope. But what does it look like to live with the final defeat of sin and death in view?

Living in light of the final death of sin means living a life of courage and hope. It means standing strong against the seductive voice of temptation. It means refusing to live for things that will soon pass away. It means giving your time, strength, resources, and skills to things that have eternal significance. And it means understanding that nothing you do in the Lord's name is ever a waste of your commitment and time.

Living with the final victory in view means living a *life* of victory as you wait for that final victory.

Read: "Therefore, my beloved brothers, be steadfast, immovable, always abounding in the work of the Lord, knowing that in the Lord your labor is not in vain." 1 CORINTHIANS 15:58

Reflect: As you think about heaven and the death of sin, what three things are you looking forward to most? Why?

---

7. What Motivates You?

If I were to view a video of the last two months of your life, what would I see? What would I note if I observed you with family members and friends, at work, in moments of leisure, and going about the mundane tasks of everyday life? What would I conclude motivates you?

The Bible teaches that we are all living for something. At the level of our hearts, there is always a reason for what we do. For example, the way you invest your free time, the things you do in your private moments, and the way you handle your money—all of these are shaped by what is important to you. We are all motivated, all of the time, by something.

The doctrine of glorification provides us with a majestic motivation for everything in our lives. Whether we are aware of it or not, the things that motivate us are often too small, too self-focused, and too temporary.

For example, when I angrily threaten my child, I am hoping that fear will get him to pick up his toys. When I honk my horn in traffic, I am hoping to motivate the drivers in front of me to move aside or drive faster. It's easy to reduce your life down to petty little moments of selfish motivation.

But future glorification is also meant to motivate us. Future glory is motivation right now, even when God has called us to make costly sacrifices. Sometimes it looks like the bad guys are winning. It can seem as though obedience simply isn't paying off. At times, suffering clouds our sense of God's presence and activity. So it's vital for us to keep our eyes on the guaranteed glory that awaits us (Ps. 73:21–24).

We have been saved by grace for something far bigger and better than a "what can I get out of this moment" way of living. We have been drawn into the family of the King of kings, the Creator and ruler of everything. We have been called to give ourselves to the work of his eternal kingdom. And we walk toward a destiny that is secure.

We cannot allow ourselves to live for what is small and temporary when we have been drawn by God into what is huge, glorious, and eternal.

Read: "When my soul was embittered, when I was pricked in heart, I was brutish and ignorant; I was like a beast toward you. Nevertheless, I am continually with you; you hold my right hand. You guide me with your counsel, and afterward you will receive me to glory." PSALM 73:21–24

Reflect: How does the glory of heaven outweigh the difficulties you may face on earth?

12

Eternity

What We Believe

God has appointed a day when Jesus Christ will judge the world. Every person who's ever lived will give an account of his or her thoughts, words, and actions— whether good or evil. God appointed this judgment day to show the glory of his mercy and also the glory of his justice. After his judgment, the righteous will be given everlasting life. The wicked, who do not know God and have not obeyed the gospel of Jesus Christ, will be thrown into eternal torment. We don't know when the Lord will come, but we should always be prepared to say, "Come, Lord Jesus, come quickly. Amen."

Why We Believe It

The passages below inform the Christian doctrine of eternity. God has spoken in the Bible, so we believe what he has said there. In the following pages, we'll explore this key doctrine and what it means for us as we follow Christ.

For God will bring every deed into judgment, with every secret thing, whether good or evil.

Ecclesiastes 12:14

Stay dressed for action and keep your lamps burning, and be like men who are waiting for their master to come home from the wedding feast, so that they may open the door to him at once when he comes and knocks. Blessed are those servants whom the master finds awake when he comes. Truly, I say to you, he will dress himself for service and have them recline at table, and he will come and serve them. If he comes in the second watch, or in the third, and finds them awake, blessed are those servants! But know this, that if the master of the house had known at what hour the thief was coming, he would not have left his house to be broken into. You also must be ready, for the Son of Man is coming at an hour you do not expect.

Luke 12:35–40

For the Father judges no one, but has given all judgment to the Son, that all may honor the Son, just as they honor the Father. Whoever does not honor the Son does not honor the Father who sent him. Truly, truly, I say to you, whoever hears my word and believes him who sent me has eternal life. He does not come into judgment, but has passed from death to life.

Truly, truly, I say to you, an hour is coming, and is now here, when the dead will hear the voice of the Son of God, and those who hear will live. For as the Father has life in himself, so he has granted the Son also to have life in himself. And he has given him authority to execute judgment, because he is the Son of Man.

John 5:22–27

What if God, desiring to show his wrath and to make known his power, has endured with much patience vessels of wrath prepared for destruction, in order to make known the riches of his glory for vessels of mercy, which he has prepared beforehand for glory.

Romans 9:22–23

Why do you pass judgment on your brother? Or you, why do you despise your brother? For we will all stand before the judgment seat of God; for it is written,

"As I live, says the Lord, every knee shall bow to me,
and every tongue shall confess to God."

So then each of us will give an account of himself to God.

Romans 14:10–12

How It Matters

Throughout this chapter, we'll focus on the Bible's teaching about eternity. Even without knowing what the Bible says about eternity, every human longs for more than this world can provide. Our hearts cry out for eternity. And God wants us to keep eternity in view as we seek to live our lives. He wants our future to shape our present. And it should—because the Christian's future is paradise, just as God has promised. Yet eternal judgment awaits everyone who rejects Christ and refuses to repent. We get too comfortable in this life, but God wants us to view life now as preparation for eternity. And in that hope, we wait—sometimes for what seems like a long time. We must keep absorbing the previews of eternity that God provides within his word—the "trailers" for the great eternity movie that will play across the universe.

1. Eternal Longing

Everyone cries out for eternity—they just don't know it.

The little boy who is choking back his tears because he has been bullied is crying out for eternity. The wife who is devastated by her husband's sin is crying out for eternity. The elderly man who is dealing with the pain, weakness, and loneliness of old age is crying out for eternity. The pastor who has ministered long with little fruit is crying out for eternity. The lonely teenager who just wants to be understood and accepted is crying out for eternity. The worker who has been yelled at by his boss once again, for reasons he doesn't understand, is crying out for eternity. The hungry homeless man is crying out for eternity. The couple who just discovered their car has been stolen is crying out for eternity.

Somehow, someway, we all know in our hearts that this world is not the way it is supposed to be. Somehow, someway, we all long for a better world.

Everything we have believed as the children of God requires a final resolution. The doctrine of eternity is essential.

Without this truth, Christianity is simply not the Christianity we gave ourselves to. Understanding this doctrine is vital if you want to understand your faith and apply it to your daily life.

Read: "He who testifies to these things says, 'Surely I am coming soon.' Amen. Come, Lord Jesus! The grace of the Lord Jesus be with all. Amen." REVELATION 22:20-21

Reflect: Where and in what ways have you recently found your heart crying out for eternity?

---

2. Live for Tomorrow

The apostle Peter writes, "Since all these things are thus to be dissolved, what sort of people ought you to be in lives of holiness and godliness" (2 Pet. 3:11).

Notice the structure of this verse: "Since . . . what . . ." It is an "if/then" sentence. If these things are true, then this is how you should live.

Peter has just said that everything around us, every single thing in this created world, will be burned up (2 Pet. 3:10). Let this sink in. Every bit of it will be gone forever. Every building, every mountain, every stream, every lush garden, every animal, every monument, every tree, every limestone cliff, every sea creature, every sandy shore, every wardrobe of fine clothes, every car, every highway, every place of solace or amusement—yes, every physical thing—will be burned up.

This physical world is not ultimate. God is ultimate, and he will bring all these things to a final and spectacular end. How? He's told us his plan in advance: The end will come in the searing heat of a final display of his glorious power.

Let's return now to Peter's question. Since this is true, what sort of lives should we live? If all of this is going to be burned up, by God's plan and his power, it's insanity to live for the physical glories of the created world. Why would I attach my identity, my meaning and purpose, and my sense of well-being to what will be gone in an instant?

No, I am not saying that you shouldn't enjoy a good steak, a fine piece of music, a great movie, or a beautiful garden. I am not saying that you shouldn't be dedicated in your job or be committed to success in school.

We are talking about what rules your heart and controls the way you live your life. Peter says that in light of the fiery end of everything around us, it only makes sense to live for the greater eternal glory of God.

Read: "Since all these things are thus to be dissolved, what sort of people ought you to be in lives of holiness and godliness, waiting for and hastening the coming of the day of God, because of which the heavens will be set on fire and dissolved, and the heavenly bodies will melt as they burn! But according to his promise we are waiting for new heavens and a new earth in which righteousness dwells." 2 PETER 3:11-13

Reflect: Where do you think your life is too attached to things of this world? How might the Lord want you to respond to his word and become less attached?

---

3. Paradise Promised

Every human being is searching for paradise. Yet there is no paradise in this fallen world. Nothing seems to fulfill our golden dreams. Nothing is as good as we wished it would be. Nothing works as we hoped it would.

We do this because we were hardwired for eternity. So Peter says, "But according to his promise we are waiting for new heavens and a new earth in which righteousness dwells" (2 Pet. 3:13). Wow, what a power-packed collection of words!

Peter is reminding us to live as if we really do believe that there is one who always does what he's promised. There is one whose words are always faithful and true. There is one who doesn't change his mind, take another direction, or turn his back on those who are waiting. There is one who never gets bored, never gets tired, and is never too busy to keep his word. And no one can stop his hand. No one.

So what is his sure and secure promise? The promise is that after the end, God is going to give us a new home. No, we won't be floating on clouds and playing golden harps. He is going to give us a new heaven and a new earth. This earth won't be like the one that we are accustomed to living in. Unlike our broken world, this will be a place where righteousness will dwell, unchallenged forever.

Nothing will ever be out of place again, fail to do its part again, or break again. Nothing will rebel against the Creator's plan. It will be a world of uninterrupted peace and harmony forever. The Bible has a name for this: *shalom*. The shalom that was shattered when Adam and Even sinned in the garden of Eden will be restored forever, never to be broken again. Perfect righteousness will reign forever and ever. This is glorious glory.

So the doctrine of eternity assures you that God will fix everything that sin has broken.

It tells you that right now you should live with that promise in mind. It warns you that physical things are not permanent. It preaches to you of the eternal importance of the way you live as you wait. And it promises you an end that is far more glorious than anything you would have dared hope for.

Read: "Henceforth there is laid up for me the crown of righteousness, which the Lord, the righteous judge, will award to me on that day, and not only to me but also to all who have loved his appearing." 2 TIMOTHY 4:8

Reflect: Where this week are you feeling the brokenness of this world? How might this reading restore your hope?

---

4. Eternal Judgment

We don't usually like to talk about hell, that place of eternal punishment. But we should. Here's why it's important. We all long for the final defeat of evil. We all cry out for a world where there is no more injustice. We all long for perfect justice to finally and forever win.

Hell tells us that evil will be defeated. Hell tells us there will be a righteous judgment. Hell tells us evil will be punished. The Bible is very clear: There will be a final judgment. And there is a real place of ultimate punishment called hell (Matt. 25:31–46).

So what is hell all about? There are three things that together create the hellishness of hell.

Separation from God. Every person—believer or unbeliever—benefits from the presence and goodness of God in this world. Imagine the awfulness of God saying, "You have wanted to live separate from me your entire life? So you will now live in that state forever." Imagine the hell of separation from God.

Inhumanity. We were not created as independent, self-sufficient human beings. We were designed to live in a loving, worshipful, and dependent relationship with God. That's how human life was meant to be lived. So what would happen if God were completely absent? If you can imagine living in this state of dark inhumanity forever, you are getting close to understanding another of the singular horrors of hell.

Unending torment. Those who will experience eternal punishment will not do so because they occasionally broke God's law, but because of a lifelong, moment-by-moment rebellion against their Creator. This is a consistent desire to be in God's place and to reject his offer of rescuing grace. The biblical description of hell's torment, its unending penalty for sin, helps us weigh the magnitude of sin's sinfulness.

It is simply impossible to gloss over what the Bible teaches about the final judgment and the eternal punishment of hell. So it is important for us to face this topic. God has revealed to us the truth of the dark side of eternity because he loves us. The threat of hell points to our need of grace.

Read: "The times of ignorance God overlooked, but now he commands all people everywhere to repent, because he has fixed a day on which he will judge the world in righteousness by a man whom he has appointed; and of this he has given assurance to all by raising him from the dead." ACTS 17:30–31

Reflect: If there were no hell, how might that change the offer of salvation? What would that say about the death of Jesus for sin?

---

5. Getting Ready

Athletes know that preparation is not as exciting as the game, but it is essential. They expect preparation to be repetitive, tiring, and painful. Yet they also know that preparation changes them.

The problem is that many of us don't have the athlete's mentality. Instead, we carry all kinds of unrealistic hopes and dreams about what this present moment will be. Then we're disappointed again and again.

Rather than living with a preparation mentality, we fall into living with a destination mentality. We live as if this is all there is. And if you live with a destination mentality, you'll ask people, places, and things to be what they will never be on this side of eternity. The results of this are never good.

But if you live with eternity in view, you won't be surprised when things don't work as they should. You'll remember that this is a time of preparation for your destination. So you won't be shocked when people are less than perfect, when your dreams don't unfold as you expected, or when hardship comes your way.

Instead, you'll know that when difficulty comes, you are being molded by the hands of the divine artist. You're being progressively shaped into something more beautiful and more fit for what is to come. Yes, you'll still experience the pain of suffering and loss, and you'll still get tired. Yet you won't experience pain without hope, exhaustion without motivation to continue, or hardship without joy.

This life is clearly not designed to be our final destination. No, this is a time of loving preparation for the glory that not only has been promised to us but also purchased for us by the willing sacrifice of our Savior.

Read: "His master said to him, 'Well done, good and faithful servant. You have been faithful over a little; I will set you over much. Enter into the joy of your master.'" MATTHEW 25:21

Reflect: Think of three hardships that you regularly face. How could you start thinking of them as preparation for your final destination?

6. Waiting for a Promised Outcome

Every child needs to understand the value of delayed gratification. Waiting simply doesn't come naturally for them. Fifteen minutes into a day-long road trip, little children ask if they're almost there. A child will go out and check for plants in the garden the day after the seeds were planted. Children haven't yet learned the simple truth that, by God's design, most good things don't happen in a moment.

The doctrine of eternity is a doctrine of delayed gratification. God's promise is sure, but so is the reality that he has chosen for us to wait. We don't disappear into the glory of eternity the moment we first believe. In God's plan, the march from the garden of Eden to the new heaven and the new earth is a slow one. In contrast, we like results to come quickly. When they don't, we get antsy and irritated. Yet the Bible teaches us that the investments we make, with eternity in view, in the little moments of our lives will have a return that will last for all of eternity.

Delayed gratification helps you to live with a patient and hopeful heart. It keeps you from demanding that all of your relationships need to be comfortable. It reminds you that your work and studies aren't always fulfilling. It helps you to be happy investing your money in things that have an eternal return rather than spending it all on present pleasure.

The doctrine of eternity reminds us that God will keep every one of his promises. Yet it also reminds us to wait with patience. In life, we'll get tastes of fulfillment along the way. However, there may be a long wait between my investment in those promises and God's final fulfillment.

This means that, even when you don't see much fruit, there is reason for hope. We don't rest our hope in how quickly God will keep his promises. Instead, we know he is always faithfully moving us to the glorious outcome that he's promised.

So with eyes on eternity—like the people of God who've gone before us—we believe, we invest, and we wait.

Read: "These all died in faith, not having received the things promised, but having seen them and greeted them from afar, and having acknowledged that they were strangers and exiles on the earth. For people who speak thus make it clear that they are seeking a homeland." HEBREWS 11:13-14

Reflect: When you feel as if you're having to wait on God to keep his promises, how do you tend to respond? Do you feel that you need to trust God more or that he needs to move faster? Why?

---

7. Keep Watching the Trailer

I think one of the greatest inventions in modern culture is the movie trailer. It gives you a taste of the plot and characters of a movie. As a result, you're able to decide whether you want to watch the movie or not.

Sometimes Luella and I decide we want to go to a movie. So I'll get out my iPad and watch movie trailers until I find the one that grabs my interest or that I think Luella will enjoy. Now, in the movie world, sometimes trailers are a bit of a lie. They show you the two gripping moments in an otherwise dull movie to make you think it's action-packed so you will buy tickets. About thirty minutes into the film, you know that you have been taken. So you sit irritated through a film that doesn't really interest you just to get your money's worth.

The doctrine of eternity is the ultimate trailer.

But it does way more than invite you into escapist entertainment for a few hours. No, this trailer welcomes you to a brand-new way of living. It pulls you back from living for momentary pleasures that soon evaporate. It warns you to live not for your own glory but for the glory of another, a glory that you will someday share face-to-face. This trailer encourages you to give yourself to something far more glorious than the trailer is able to display.

But here's the problem: Everything in the eternity trailer challenges the way we actually think and live.

So here's what you and I have to do. We have to keep watching the eternity trailer over and over again. You won't find it on online. Yet you will find it starting with the first page of Genesis and propelling you to the last chapter of Revelation. You and I have to dive into this narrative day after day. And God designed this eternity trailer to be transformative.

God has given us the trailer. It's ours not just to casually think about but to take in and consume. At first, things around us may seem to stay the same. Yet over time, by God's grace, we will change and the way we live will change. We just have to keep watching the trailer.

Read: "For this light momentary affliction is preparing for us an eternal weight of glory beyond all comparison, as we look not to the things that are seen but to the things that are unseen. For the things that are seen are transient, but the things that are unseen are eternal."
2 CORINTHIANS 4:17–18

Reflect: What aspect of eternity has begun to captivate your heart more and more? How has that happened in your life? How can you continue to stoke that fire?

Scripture Index

Genesis
book of....................156
1...............................60, 74, 77, 84
1:1.............................19, 74
1:1–5.........................69
1:3.............................60
1:11...........................60
1:20...........................60
1:21...........................60
1:26...........................89
1:26–28.....................81
1:27...........................84
2................................74, 77
2:7.............................85
2:16–17.....................93
3................................48
3:6.............................64

Exodus
34:6–7.......................15

Numbers
11:23.........................57
23:19.........................47

1 Samuel
2:2.............................29

1 Chronicles
16:31.........................49
29:11–13....................19

2 Chronicles
20:6...........................18

Nehemiah
9:6.............................69

Psalms
8:5–6.........................89
19:1...........................22
19:1–11.....................4
19:7...........................7
27..............................24
27:7–8.......................25
32:1–5.......................105
36:9...........................8
51:1–5.......................93
51:4...........................98
73:21–24....................143
86:11.........................8
95:6...........................77
99:5...........................34
102:25–27...................23
104:24–25...................69
119:97–99...................9
119:104–105...............11
119:105......................11
119:130......................6
135:6.........................43
139:13–14...................73

Ecclesiastes
7:29...........................87
12:14.........................147

Isaiah

6	36
6:1–3	35
6:1–7	30
6:3	33
6:5	36
6:6–7	36
6:8–9	36
14:27	60
40:25	32
40:28	20
40:29	65
43:15	35
44:6–8	57
45:7	50
45:9	50
46:10–11	43
53:5–6	105
55	38
55:10–11	38
55:13	38
57:15	30
61:1	100

Jeremiah

32:17	57
32:27	46
32:40	136

Ezekiel

36:26	101

Daniel

4:34–35	44

Micah

7:18–20	15

Nahum

1:2–3	16

Matthew

6:31–33	51
8:23–27	58
10:29–31	48
23:23	90
25:21	154
25:31–46	152

Mark

14:36	66

Luke

1:37	64
6:43–45	94
12:35–40	147

John

1:1–3	70
1:14–18	16
5:22–27	148
6:37–40	137
8:34	99
10:27–30	137
10:29	137
16:8	128
16:12–14	4
16:13	128
17:17	39
17:20–23	113

Acts

17:26–28	82
17:30–31	153
20:32	122

Romans

1:20	78
2:14–15	87
3:21–28	106
4:5–8	109
5:12–17	94
5:18–19	97
6:1–2	124
6:16	100
6:19	119
7:24–8:1	98
8:26	129
8:28	52, 136
8:28–30	136
8:28–39	135
8:29–30	52, 135
8:31–32	115, 136
8:35–39	136
9:22–23	148
11:33–36	16
11:36	75
13:1	77
14:10–12	148

1 Corinthians

1:18–31	7

158 **SCRIPTURE INDEX**

1:30–31	112
2:7–9	140
6:19–20	76
8:6	75
9:24	138
13	86
15:55–57	142
15:58	142

2 Corinthians

3:18	90
4:17–18	156
5:1–8	133
7:1	126
10:4–5	124
12:10	63

Galatians

book of	112
2:20	112, 113
6:9	138

Ephesians

1:3–14	44
1:4	111
1:17–19	129
1:19–23	63
2:4–5	96
2:8–9	110
3:14–19	119
3:20–21	61
4:11–16	126
4:15–16	119
4:23–32	82

Philippians

3:8–9	106
3:12–13	123

Colossians

1:16–18	70
3:1–4	124
3:2–4	88

2 Thessalonians

2:14	133

1 Timothy

3	126
3:14–15	127

2 Timothy

2:10–13	134
3:14–17	4
4:8	152

Hebrews

2:1	10
2:14–15	102
3:12–13	99
10:12	108
10:36	138
11:3	74
11:6	21
11:13–14	155
12:1	139
12:14	120

James

1:2–4	128
3:8–10	82
4:1–4	100, 101
4:13–15	49

1 Peter

1:3–5	134
1:15–16	30
2:11	120
5:10–11	53

2 Peter

1:19–21	4
3:10	150
3:11	150
3:11–13	151
3:13	151

1 John

3:1	114
3:1–10	134
3:2	140, 141
4:8	86

Revelation

book of	156
1:8	62
3:11	138
4:8	30
4:11	72
15:4	37
22:3	141
22:20–21	150

PAUL TRIPP MINISTRIES

Paul Tripp Ministries is a not-for-profit organization connecting the transforming power of Jesus Christ to everyday life. Supported by generous donors, they make much of Paul's gospel teaching freely available online, on podcasts, across social media, and in the Paul Tripp app.

PaulTripp.com

/pdtripp   @paultripp   @paultrippquotes
@pauldavidtripp   /add/pauldavidtripp   /in/paul-david-tripp/

Also Available from Paul David Tripp

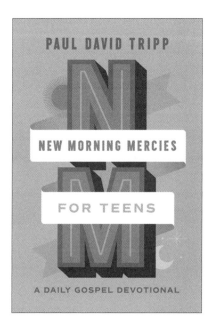

"For many years, Tripp has shaped our own lives, family, and ministry through his biblical wisdom, generous friendship, and wonderful way with words. Now, as the parents of four daughters, we are thrilled for our girls to receive the same blessing of biblical truth, beautifully distilled in devotional form, that speaks to the joys and fears, delights and concerns, questions and hopes of their growing hearts."

KEITH AND KRISTYN GETTY
hymn writers and recording artists, "In Christ Alone"; authors, *Sing! How Worship Transforms Your Life, Family, and Church*

For more information, visit **crossway.org** or **paultripp.com**.